Your Residence in Paradise

Your Residence in Paradise

Global Property Purchase—Example Florida

Andrea Hoff-Domin

1. Edition 2014—English
2. Edition 2016 – English updated

Photographs by Florida Dream Homes Realty LLC

Map by Microsoft map point

Logos by the National Association of Realtors

Cover photograph by Microsoft Office

ISBN: 0986252913

ISBN-13: 978-0986252914

Dedication

This book is dedicated to my godmother in my birth country. She was always there to help when I needed her. She always has an open ear for me and open arms for a loving hug.

About the Author

Born on October 6 in lower Saxony, Germany, Andrea Hoff-Domin lost her father when she was a baby, and life with her new stepfather was never easy. Books about foreign countries and their culture were her escape from everyday life and inspired her enthusiasm for the wide world. Her grandparents, especially her grandfather, had a big influence on her. He was an architect, and she accompanied him on his trips to construction sites and sat at his feet when he was drawing houses. At that time, she developed her passion for houses and properties, which is her main profession today.

She runs an international brokerage in Florida and is known as a Florida expert. To fulfill her lifelong dream, she started her career as a financial specialist in the biggest German bank and renovated condominiums. During that time, she began to write for several magazines and Internet portals. She lives by the motto "Do or do not; there is no try" (Yoda, Star Wars).

www.florida-dream-homes.net
www.andreahoffdomin.com
andrea@florida-informations.com

Contents

You Only Live Once—Make the Most of It!

A few years ago, there was a television advertisement from a large bank in Germany, where I was born, with the slogan "my house, my boat, my horse, my wife." The advertising bank showed lovely pictures of a nice home in a tropical environment, a big yacht on the open sea, a beautiful racing horse, and his lovely wife. The motivation for this advertisement is certainly clear: the bank was looking for new customers for their products, especially in-house savings products that would allow customers to afford nice things like these in the future. Think about it. Wouldn't it be nice to have a house or condominium in a nice tropical area where the water at the beach is warm and the sun is always shining?

Wouldn't it be great to have a property with a boat somewhere where life is interesting and the weather is warm? The sun shines every day from the sky. The private pool glistens in the backyard and invites you to jump in. This refreshing water is only a stone's throw away. In this tropical environment, palm trees swing slowly in the wind and the smooth breeze caresses your skin. Doesn't that sound heavenly to you?

In such tropical surroundings, a boat is a common accessory for a house, and the best part is that the boat is often waiting in your own backyard at your private dock. When you listen closely, you can hear the ocean calling for you and inviting you to your next trip on the ocean.

You may think this is not affordable—that it is only a dream. But our dreams are our best inspiration in life, and we can make them come true. We only have to dream this dream, and with passion and persistence, we will find the solution to realize our dreams. This is my experience, and I strive every day for my dreams and my goals.

Maybe you are asking yourself, How? And where? And most importantly, what will it this amazing dream cost? Is it safe, or is it a fragile soap bubble and I will lose my money? What is the catch? Will someone cheat me?

Do you have the courage to follow your dreams? Then you should keep on reading and find out for yourself how you can make your dreams come true. First, you have already invested in the book in your hands to fulfill your dream, and second, you will try to avoid the possible pitfalls and obstacles on your way to your dream. In addition, with the tips and tricks in this book, you will save a lot of money, which you can invest into your new dream home or in a new hobby—perhaps your new boat. There are many beautiful things to explore and conquer.

The ideas and details presented in this book are written from the perspective of a licensed Real Estate Broker. The information is focused on the purchase of a property in a foreign country and its investment return. A Florida real estate transaction is used as an example for this topic.

Why Florida? It is the ideal spot to live your life in paradise, and your investment is as safe as it is at home in your home country.

The Sunshine State of Florida is located in the United States and is a magnet in the international real estate business. Due to its pleasant climate and its lifestyle, Florida is one of the best known and most popular living and vacation destinations in the world.

When you buy a property in Florida, you are moving into the international real estate business.

Properties in Florida are governed by the property laws of the United States and Florida, and these laws apply to all property owners—US citizens as well as non–US citizens. The laws are beneficiary and lucrative for all. The money transfer to the United States is easy and secure. The economic situation is stable and growing.

In this book, you will learn fascinating facts and useful information that will make your dream of "Your Residence in Paradise" come true. However, please keep in mind that this book is not a "do-it-yourself" guide.

The international real estate market is very different from that in your home country. These differences are varied and should not be underestimated.

Also, no property is like another. Each dream house has its own hidden treasures, and each has its benefits. This book explains and describes the most important information and details that will help you selecting the right dream home and make your purchase transaction successful.

There is no homogeneous property market, and there is not only one price for a house. Each neighborhood (residential district) and every town and county (region) has its own charm and its own micro–real estate market. There is something interesting for everyone. It is important to find just the right and special dream home for you.

In order to find this gem in the haystack, you need to contact a local, competent, and experienced real estate specialist. Only he or she will have the necessary knowledge and experience to help you to find what you are looking for.

"But," you may be asking, "does that cost a lot of money?"

On the contrary. The right local broker or agent will help you find your dream home and can also save you a lot of money when you buy. They can help you to earn more money with the home in the future.

Perhaps you don't believe this because your experience with brokers in your home country has not been positive. There are many responses to this. A local broker or agent in the United States knows all the necessary details of your dream home and often speaks your language as well. Many real estate professionals have foreign ancestors. For you as a buyer, their services are free, because the cost is paid by the seller of the property.

Well, are you curious yet? Then let us start and jump into your project!

"Your Residence in Paradise".

Live Your Dream in Florida

Maybe you are wondering, why Florida? Why not Spain or South France or Mexico, for example, or any other country that lies just beyond the border of your home country?

Quite simply, I am living in Florida for years. The Sunshine State offers many attractions, beautiful tropical landscapes, and nature reserves. Animals that you may only know from a visit to the zoo are your neighbors and will visit your yard regularly.

Florida is a very safe state—not only in terms of your personal safety, but also safe for your investment. The real estate property rights are strict and protect the homeowner. In your home country, property rights for foreign nationals may be very different from those in the United States. You cannot rely on your legal understanding of how transactions work in your own country.

The property market in the United States, and particularly in Florida, is stable and currently still favorable for property investments. You can still find a real estate treasure there.

Before we dive into the real estate market, let us see why Florida may be the land of dreams for you. Let us explore this tropical paradise.

Florida, known as the Sunshine State, is quite diverse and has something for everyone. The most important point is that you take the first step and make your dreams come true. The second and any further steps are much easier and will happen like magic. Believe me, you will like being in Florida.

I also want to clear up some stereotypes about Florida that you might have heard of.

The media—television, newspapers, and magazines—are usually quick at hand with sensational reports and matching images, but these pictures do not always show the reality.

Stories that feature great damage and many injuries and deaths are better selling points than pictures in which the people living in that area are helping each other. That is reality too. However, the media do not like that and therefore prefer not to show such pictures.

In the case of a natural disaster, you will learn to know the real kindness and sense of community of Americans. Everyone helps everyone without exception. They stick together no matter what.

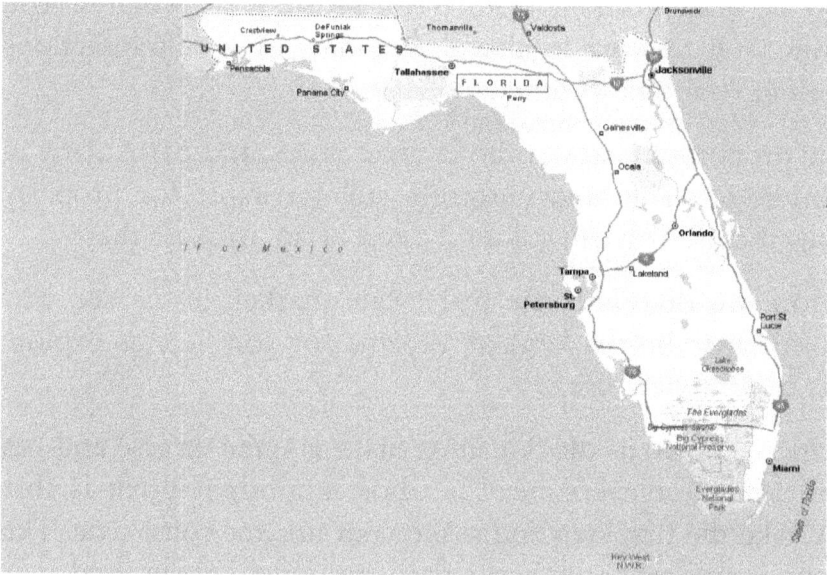

Florida—The Southernmost Point of the United States

Since March 3, 1845, the state of Florida has been a part of the United States. From its annexation to the United States until the start of railway construction at the end of the nineteenth century, Florida existed quietly because the potential of this state was not yet detected. Railroad magnate Henry Flagler discovered the benefits of the state as a holiday paradise in the 1890s.

He built his first railway line from New York to West Palm Beach. This was the starting point for the development of Florida as a vacation paradise. Along his railway, he built large hotels where tourists from northern states spent their winter vacations each year. The Sunshine State of Florida was born and became a recreation paradise.

This vacation paradise was initially only affordable for the rich and super rich, who escaped the cold, snowy winter months here in the south. They behaved like birds that moved every year to the south to escape the cold temperatures.

This human travel behavior has increased until today, and nowadays these visitors have their own nick name: they are the "snowbirds," and they start their journey south every year in late October.

The last stop of the first railway line into the south was West Palm Beach. From there, a traveler who wanted to travel farther south had to either take the arduous route through the swamps on bumpy roads or use the existing shipping route to Cutler Bay in the south of Miami, or to Key West.

The first settlements in southern Florida were Fort Lauderdale, Miami, and Key West. Miami and Fort Lauderdale were initially postal and commercial stations for the settlers and eventually developed into today's modern metro areas. The connection between these outposts was steady growing with increasing speed.

Flagler's dream of building the first railroad along the east coast of the United States, from New York to Key West, came later. In 1912, shortly before his death, Flagler's dream was realized and his railroad was completed. That was the first connection from the mainland to the southernmost point of the United States, Key West.

Until that time, the former pirate's nest was only accessible by boat. Because of its isolated location, Key West has been, since its inception, something special. This specialty and the particular flair of the place is still alive, and its pirate-filled past is cherished until today.

With the completion of the railroad to Key West, the entire east coast of the Sunshine State could be reached easily from the mainland and the northern states. The development of the vacation paradise and winter residence grew and continues to increase today.

The railroad to Key West existed until 1935. A hurricane on September 2, 1935, destroyed parts of the railway and washed it away. The remains of this old railroad are preserved as monuments and can be seen when traveling by car to Key West.

It was too costly to rebuild the railroad, so it was replaced with a road—the federal highway US Highway 1. This road ends right in the middle of Key West.

This road, also called the Overseas Highway, is the artery to Key West on which all goods are transported and all visitors come into town. The ride to Key West on this highway, with its many bridges, is an experience that you should not miss. It is a highlight on a discovery trip to Florida.

Since those early beginnings, Florida has secured its position as the number-one vacation and travel spot. Tourism, along with its related industries like the cruise industry, hotels, and restaurants, are still the main economic industries in the state.

However, more and more other industries have moved into the state and bring new employment options with them. These new businesses are in the health, medical, and space research industries and have a positive impact on the economic development of the Sunshine State.

New businesses are not only from the United States. Many foreign companies that have discovered Florida as a business location come from all over the world. This makes Florida economically more independent from tourism.

A few years ago, for example, the Max Planck Institute from Germany established a research center in West Palm Beach.

MANY, MANY QUESTIONS ABOUT FLORIDA...

This short excursion has certainly made you curious, and the first questions about the book's topic are at the tip of your tongue. We cannot have a face-to-face conversation, of course. However, my professional experience and the constant contact with my customers has provided me with a long list of questions that may come into your mind when you think about your real estate dreams.

Surely one or more of these questions will also be in your head, and the answer will help you make the right decision about how to realize your dream.

With the right information and facts, your life's dream "Your Residence in Paradise," will come true.

Is Florida an Interesting Second Home Spot for You?

There are many answers to this question, and for me the answer may be different than it is for you. I do not know your priorities for a vacation paradise; I can only speak from my point of view and hope that it will match with yours.

For me, lifestyle and fun in life is very important. Therefore, we focus on these parts of life. In this areas, Florida is at the top of the list.

The weather, the water, and the endless long beaches make Florida into a paradise whose like you will hardly find anywhere else on the planet.

The weather is a highlight in this state. The sun shines nearly every day. The sky is blue with fluffy clouds. At the coast, you often have a nice breeze from the ocean that creates a comfortable climate. The water is clear and warm, and waves roll smoothly onto the sandy beach.

The average temperature on the state level is twenty-eight degrees Celsius during the day and twenty degrees at night. During the winter, temperatures rarely fall below fifteen degrees at night, and twenty-four degrees in the daytime is normal. Based on these numbers, winter temperatures are comparable to average summer temperatures in Germany. To get your own impression about the climate, please compare these facts to your own temperatures at home.

At these temperatures and in this subtropical climate, there is often a slight wind blowing that creates a pleasant cooling feeling. The typical Florida home uses this natural cooling like a natural air conditioner.

Nearly all properties have some sort of air-conditioning system inside to maintain comfortable temperatures indoors. To cool off quickly after an active day, you have your swimming pool in the back yard, and one of the biggest bathtubs in the world, the Atlantic Ocean, is not far away.

The sky varies in color from baby blue to rich blue. When the sun sinks into the sea in the evening, the horizon shows countless shades of red. Such moments are best enjoyed with a glass of champagne in your hand at the beach.

Another highlight is Florida's location. The Sunshine State is a peninsula surrounded on three sides by open waters. This location gives Florida one of the longest coastlines in the United States, and the many beaches are the hallmarks of the Sunshine State.

On the east coast is the Atlantic Ocean, whose waves are great for surfers and kite surfers. Life and entertainment pulses vigorously in the southern cities of Miami and Fort Lauderdale.

The Gulf of Mexico on the west coast of the peninsula is quiet. Waves lap softly here on the beach. On this side of the peninsula, everything is quiet and contemplative.

To use a comparison, Gulf of Mexico on the west coast corresponds to the Baltic Sea or the Mediterranean in Europe, while the east coast is equivalent to the North Sea with its waves and tides.

If you are a water, beach, and sun lover, then Florida is exactly the right place for you to enjoy your life to the fullest.

What Makes Florida So Attractive?

I do not know where you are living, so I can only offer my point of view. For Europeans who come from the moderate climate zone, Florida is a sun and vacation paradise that offers something for everyone, with its entertainment, beaches, and water.

Florida does not give you vague promises of summer. Here is summer the whole year round. The sun shines from the sky throughout the year, including the winter months.

When in Europe, fur hats, long scarves, winter coats, and boots are necessary, but in Florida you will need at most a cardigan in the evening, when the evening breeze is getting a little crisp. Otherwise, T-shirts, lightweight pants, and swimwear with flip-flops are the dress code. The life motto is easygoing and live and let live.

Besides the water and beaches, Florida offers many other activities and attractions. Florida is known for its tennis courts and its many golf courses.

In the cities, museums and art galleries attract visitors. In addition, many cities organize festivals and events where you can learn a lot about the country and people.

Trips that involve hiking and bird-watching in the state's many nature parks are highlights of the quieter lifestyle.

For entertainment lovers, Orlando is just right, with its many amusement parks.

Those who love science and space will find in Cape Canaveral and the Kennedy Space Center the ultimate adventure.

These are only a few of the highlights that await you here in Florida, and there are new ones coming every day. You will not be bored.

Are the Temperatures Comfortable?

Because of Florida's location, the temperature never drops below zero degrees Celsius in most parts of the state. At the southern tip of the peninsula, the temperatures are always in the two-digit positive range. In winter, the Florida temperatures are comparable to the temperatures of a moderately warm summer in Europe.

The average temperature in the north of the state is approximately twenty-six degrees Celsius, while the temperature in the south is two degrees higher.

The temperatures at night in the northern part of the state are about fourteen degrees Celsius on average, while in the south the temperature does not drop below twenty degrees. So the temperatures are warm throughout the year.

The annual average water temperatures are twenty-three to twenty-seven degrees Celsius.

The measurement of the temperatures is described in Celsius, but temperatures are measured and reported in Fahrenheit in Florida. A water temperature of twenty-three degrees Celsius equals 73.4 Fahrenheit, and the air temperature of twenty-six degrees Celsius corresponds to 78.8 Fahrenheit.

This pleasant temperature is the most important reason that many visitors come to Florida in the winter—they want to escape their own colder climates. These visitors often enjoy six months in the southern Florida sun.

They do it like the birds that fly south through the winter. This travel behavior gave them the loving name of "snowbird." Every year in October and November, they come like birds to Florida and stay until March and April.

Many of these snowbirds have their own little nests that they inhabit during their winter stay, and in the summer they rent it and receive income that helps cover the expenses for the maintenance of the property.

In summer, temperatures in Florida are indeed warmer, but the sea breeze that blows continuously is pleasantly refreshing.

The different climate-control systems in Florida properties also provide comfortable house temperatures during the summer time.

Even if the sky sometimes weeps a little bit, these raindrops are warm, and they give you a feeling of a light refreshing shower. The rain showers are usually short and heavy, and the sun comes back quickly.

What Kinds of Water Activities Does Florida Offer?

Water temperatures in Florida are warm year round, almost like a big bathtub. The rolling ocean waves at the beach can be very soothing and relaxing in the clear, salty air.

The Atlantic Ocean beach, with its ocean waves, provides an ideal environment for hang gliders and body surfers. Also water scooters and boaters as well as anglers can get their enjoyment in and at the waters.

For diving enthusiasts, there is a lot to discover. Especially off the eastern coast of Florida, there are numerous shipwrecks from the colonial ages. The coral reefs along the shore, with their many interesting fish and other sea creatures, invite you to experience the underwater world.

To visit the shipwrecks, you usually need a small boat. However, in Fort Lauderdale and Pompano Beach, some sunken ships lie so close to the beaches that good swimmers can get to the wrecks directly from the beach. Just a few days ago, I watched some divers who returned from their discovery dive at the beach.

If swimming is not your thing, perhaps you would enjoy deep sea fishing. You can easily rent a boat and go on a fishing trip. Or do as friends of mine did and rent a boat for your own private and intimate cruise on the ocean.

Nature lovers will enjoy boat trips to the offshore natural parks. In these parks, you can rent kayaks and paddle boats and go on your own personal discovery tour or you can use the many excursion boats.

In a glass-bottom boat, you can go to the reef that is located off the coast of Florida. When you arrive at the reef, the glass-bottom boat will cruise over the reef and allow you a safe view into the underwater world of the reef through the glass hull.

There, you will not only see different types of corals and fish, but also manta rays and sharks. If you met such creatures underwater, you would not want to cross paths with them, but here you can watch them safely from the surface.

Want to conquer the reef on your own? You might want to consider joining a diving trip. If you're lucky, you might meet dolphins and manatees on your diving expedition.

Sometimes you will even have the chance to swim together with the curious dolphins. In case you meet manatees, please keep an appropriate distance from these animals. Manatees are a protected species and may only be observed but not touched. Touching a manatee is a criminal offense and will be prosecuted.

Please take this seriously:
only watching—no touching.

What Is So Special About the Beaches in Florida?

Due to its enormous coastline, Florida has countless beaches. The beaches are open to the public, and many are in conservation areas.

Based on location, the widths of the beaches vary, and they have different textures. The beaches in the natural preserves are kept in their primordial state. That means that these are often not sandy beaches but pebble or coral stone beaches. At such beaches, flip-flops or beach slippers are recommended.

The beaches near the tourist centers and cities have fine white sand. These beaches also have lifeguard stations like those in the TV series Baywatch with David Hasselhoff.

At these lifeguard stations, you can get the actual daily water temperatures and times of the tides as well as warnings for dangerous water currents and sea creatures that are close to the beach.

The dangerous currents are called "rip currents" in Florida. They develop when the wind pushes the water toward the beach. When the water flows back, it creates a funnel-shaped channel with the dangerous current. When you get caught in this flow channel, you will not be able to reach the beach by swimming directly toward shore. The water will pull you into the sea, even if you are an experienced swimmer. You should absolutely avoid such flows.

You will often hear about rip current warnings in the morning while having coffee and watching the news. In this case the best plan is not to go to the lifeguard station on the beach. Just go directly to the shopping mall.

When you are enjoying the beach, the soft sea breeze will cool you a little. It's not only refreshing, but it also blows the rain clouds away.

At the beach in Florida during spring or summer, you will notice wooden pegs and straps surrounding various areas. These areas are marine turtle nests. The nests are protected, and it is prohibited to enter these areas until the baby turtles have left their nests and moved into the vast ocean world.

What Can You Do in Florida Besides Going to the Beach?

Beach, waves, sun, and water are the most important things in Florida. However, all the other attractions should not be forgotten.

Tennis

Florida has several high-class international tennis events every year, such as the Tournament of Key Biscayne. This event attracts many contestants and visitors. Even if you do not belong to the tennis elite, you will have the opportunity to compete throughout the year in various tennis tournaments with others. Many of these tournaments are on the east coast and in the south of the Sunshine State.

For the average tennis player, there are many public tennis courts available in the cities. Their use is sometimes free of charge or may cost only a small fee. There are also private tennis courts in many communities.

Golf

Golf is another major sport in Florida. Golf courses are all over Florida, but the main areas for professional golfers are Central and North Florida.

The well-known international PGA tournaments in Florida are played in Palm Beach and Miami.

If you are a golf enthusiast who wants to go every day on the green and play your golf round, then you have many private golf clubs to choose from. However, the game fees in these clubs are usually expensive if you are not a member.

A cheaper alternative to paying for a club membership is to play at one of the many public golf courses in the municipalities. These golf courses have moderate fees and often offer special deals.

Nature Reserves

The United States is very active in environment and wildlife protection and sets high standards for its national parks. The most important and largest national park in the Sunshine State is located in South Florida. It is called Everglades National Park.

Also called the river of grass, this nature reserve is located on the southwest tip of the Florida peninsula, and its boundary extends to the north of Lake Okeechobee in Palm Beach.

In this nature reserve is also the Big Cypress Nature Park, where the Seminoles have their homeland.

Other national parks include the Biscayne National Park in the southern area of Miami and the Dry Tortugas.

The Dry Tortugas is a group of islands that are located west of Key West. These islands are only accessible by plane or boat.

Another important national park is the Canaveral National Park in the northeast part of the state. Within the boundaries of the park is the NASA site with its spaceship launch pads.

The NASA site is a military area, and therefore parts of the park have restricted access and are not open to the public.

Amusement Parks

If you have children or you have kept your inner child, then you are in the right place. You have the capital of entertainment in Florida right around the corner: Orlando.

On October 1, 1971, the Walt Disney World complex opened its doors. Plans had already started secretly in the late 60s to acquire an appropriately large area so that the growth of the park to today's existing size was possible.

The first Disney parks, Magic Kingdom and Epcot, were a great success right from the beginning, and many other amusement parks emerged nearby. The best known and most visited parks besides Disney World are the Universal Park, Wet 'n' Wild, Discovery Cove, and Legoland.

In the evening, you have many entertainment options besides the Pleasure Island and the Universal Walk. At these two parks, there are several evening music events and restaurant events. It is nearly impossible to be bored in Orlando.

Museums and Historic Sites

There are many historical buildings in the cities leftover from Florida's founding days. These remaining buildings are often not at their original construction sites. Often these buildings have been transported to historical places to be united with other historical buildings. At such a places, you get a much better feeling for the atmosphere of the past.

These historic buildings are often home to local exhibitions with authentic photos and documents. Some examples in Fort Lauderdale are the Stranahan House and the historic buildings in the Downtown Area.

Florida is also home to many major museums with nationwide contents and exhibits:

- The Florida History Museum in Tallahassee

- The National Aviation Museum in Pensacola

- The South Florida Museum in Tampa

- The Museum of Art and the Museum of Discovery and Science in Fort Lauderdale

- The Villa Vizcaya in Miami

This list is only a small selection of the many museums in the Sunshine State.

Wellness and Health

The topic of wellness, health, and life balance is very important in Florida. Everybody knows that we are not only living for work, we also need sufficient recreation and relaxation to stay healthy. And relaxation is a big business here.

There are many spa and wellness businesses throughout Florida. In the tourist centers in South Florida, these day spas are usually connected with the hotels and resorts. These hotels offer their wellness services not only to the guests of the hotels but to paying "outsiders" as well.

Native Americans

Did you enjoy reading books about cowboys and Indians or watching Western movies growing up? Then you are at the right place here in Florida, where you have the best opportunity to learn something about the real lives of Native Americans.

There are two tribes in Florida, the Seminole and the Miccosukee. Their settlement area—the reservation—is located in Central and South Florida. In these settlements you will get a deep insight view into their culture and their history.

The Native Americans have full autonomy within their reservation. That means they have the power of law enforcement and their own education and health system.

The Seminole and Miccosukee are very good at business, and they are totally different in economic terms from the stereotypes that are often portrayed in the media. Their main sources of income are the casinos on their reservations, cattle breeding, and tourism.

Casinos

In most states, casino gambling is illegal or only permitted in a very limited capacity. After Utah, Florida is the next state in which casino gambling is an important industry.

Most casinos are in South Florida in the tourist centers, and they are mostly operated by the Seminole and Miccosukee tribes.

The casinos are sort of local entertainment centers. You cannot only gamble at tables and slot machines, but you can also bet on horses and dogs. When you get hungry, you have several restaurants, bars, and bistros to choose from. There are also often concerts and musical events of well-known artists in the casino. A visit to a casino is always interesting.

Gay Scene

Florida has one of the most vibrant gay scenes in the country. It is to foreign nationals sometimes a little bit unusual how openly this issue is dealt with in the Sunshine State, but for Floridians this topic is normal.

Until the end of 2014, gay marriage was illegal in Florida, but since January 2, 2015, gays and lesbians have the legal right to marry. This decision was celebrated by the gay community and was followed by a wave of marriage requests in many cities.

There are many gay communities in all of the major cities, but the largest is in South Florida. Sometimes they are concentrated in one area of the county, such as Oakland Park in Broward.

Other cities with large gay communities include Key West, Fort Lauderdale, and Miami. In case you are interested, you can request more information from us by email. Please find the email address at the end of the book.

What About Hurricanes?

Everyone knows that there are hurricanes in Florida. Hurricane season starts on June 1 and ends on November 30 each year. Floridians have learned to live with this climate condition, because in most years it presents no major problem.

The last major hurricane on the east coast of Florida was Wilma in October 2005, and since that hurricane many things have changed regarding storm protection and preparedness.

There is a national severe weather warning system in place, and everyone knows the necessary precautions to life and limb. In event of a storm, the Community Emergency Response Team (these are volunteers from the fire department) helps older and disabled people evacuate and brings these people to safety. The members of CERT also support the fire department and the police in their duties and are trained in first aid and life rescue.

Believe me, I am already living several years in Florida and have witnessed several storms, but what you see in the media—houses flying over your head and the like—is greatly exaggerated.

Other countries also experience severe weather phenomena.

In summer 2014, for example, my business partner told me that in Germany they had severe storms that crippled the entire inner cities for days.

Let us come back to the "flying houses" in Florida These are mostly trailer homes and mobile homes that were either not properly secured for a hurricane or improperly maintained. Such homes are easy game for a storm.

Homeowners in Florida are obligated to secure the property either with hurricane-proof windows and doors or with sufficiently strong hurricane shutters.

The two kinds of hurricane shutters include accordion shutters, which can easily be closed in the event of a storm, or aluminum panels that are mounted over windows and doors.

Florida also passed stronger roof construction requirements in its building codes as well. With these new requirements, owners will not only protect their homes but will also receive a discount on their homeowner's insurance if the new codes are followed.

Through training and information brochures, each resident knows the emergency measures to apply in the event of a hurricane and what foods and supply items to buy and keep in the house. When you go shopping just before a storm, you might not be able to get what you need because the shelves will already be empty.

During hurricane season, the weather is observed in the Atlantic and Gulf of Mexico, and as soon as a tropical turbulence forms, this distruptance will be closely monitored by aircraft and satellites. Any changes will be evaluated, and

Floridians will be informed accordingly in the news.

For a dangerous storm, there is a five-day warning time. Within this time frame, hurricane preparations need to be completed and family and/or friends should be informed of where you are going to be during the storm. This helps with the search in case you get lost during the storm.

What Does Florida Have to Offer?

Florida offers something for everyone who loves very much sun and fun in life. In your everyday life, you only need to be open-minded and a little bit curious, and you must have the courage to explore your new environment in Florida. Floridians will give you kindness and tolerance and will invite you into their community.

The diversity of Florida has something for everyone. This state is the junction between South and North America, and the different cultures melt together into a colorful mix. This potpourri combines American business expertise with South American joie de vivre.

The farther south you are in Florida, the more Latin-American flair you will find in all life areas. You'll find an easygoing atmosphere with parties in the evening after successful business days. Restaurants and bars offer a wide range of entertainment.

To the north, the lifestyle is more strongly influenced by old Southern charm, and the North American lifestyle replaces more and more the South American way of life.

A private home in your favorite location is the best way to

enjoy this colorful and rich life to the fullest. Whether you want to choose a house or a condo depends on your personal preferences and goals. You will learn in the course of this book how to make the right decision for you.

Florida is interesting not only for individuals of all ages, but also to businesspeople. As a business location, Florida is an excellent choice because of the existing tax laws and the well-educated work force.

What Does Florida Offer to Seniors?

With its mild climate, the state of Florida is an ideal place for seniors to live. The term senior does not have negative connotations in the United States. It only indicates that a person has an advanced life experience.

In the United States, a person is considered a senior after the age of fifty. At that age, you will receive a special insurance card or a discount card that grants you benefits in many areas of daily life. In addition to a discount on insurance, you'll also get discounts on travel and hotel bookings, restaurants, pharmacies, and much more.

When turning fifty-five, seniors have the option to live in one of the many "55+" communities in Florida. These housing complexes contain nearly everything that is important for active, aging people.

These residential complexes are not assisted-living facilities. Their residents are self-sufficient and live independently. Many of them are also still working or at least volunteer actively in the community.

The opportunities in these residential communities include games like Bingo, exercise classes, entertainment, and medical care.

For short trips, there are usually small shuttle buses available to take the residents to the nearest shopping center or to the nearest casino if they do not own a car or just do not want to drive on their own.

The many local museums, art galleries, and attractions in the surrounding area have a lot to offer and provide additional variety and entertainment.

There is certainly something for everyone. Even for a foreign national senior.

What Does Florida Offer to Families?

For families with children, Florida is a vacation oasis. There are many attractions for young and old. All attractions are well signposted and can be quickly and conveniently reached from the branched road network. The annoying parking problem does not exist, because there are sufficient parking spaces available everywhere.

The most famous attractions in Florida are the amusement parks in Orlando, in the center of Florida. In the early '70s, they were built on former swampland. The first entertainment complex was Walt Disney World. Later, other parks were built, like the Universal Studios park and many more.

Each park has its own special adventure to discover. With your children, you can make a new discovery or experience every day.

Of course, there is more for families in Florida than Orlando with its many amusement parks. There are also lots of local attractions with their nature and water activities that you should not underestimate. Even if you do not have a house on or close to the beach, you can usually reach a beach in about fifteen to twenty minutes in the coastal areas.

The beach offers everything—swimming, diving, fishing, kite flying, surfing, building sand castles, and collecting shells.

Another possibility is exploring the Everglades and the Keys with the many animal and nature reserves. These are easy and quick to reach, and park rangers can provide lots of interesting information and guidance about the wildlife, landscape, and history.

Maybe you and your children want to get acquainted with the culture of the Native Americans. The Miccosukee and Seminole tribes are happy to invite you into their reservations. There you will learn a lot about the true story of the Native Americans, who used to be called the Indians.

If you are in South Florida at the right time, you may have even a chance to attend the big Pow Wow, a nationwide dance festival and rodeo. You can imagine yourself back into the times of the Old West and experience Native American culture firsthand.

What About Singles or Couples Without Children?

Singles and couples who come here will have fun too. The colorful party scene, especially in Miami Beach, is not only a magnet for models, fashion agencies, designers, and artists. Everybody who is or wants to be hip gathers here.

Along Ocean Boulevard in Miami Beach, there is always party at night. The many bars, bistros, restaurants, and cafes lure with exotic cocktails and live music, to end the day in the mild evening air.

Another party area is Bayfront Park in downtown Miami. This area is known for its live concerts and events such as the Red Bull Flugtag.

For fans of the Miami Heat basketball team, the American Airlines Arena is right next to Bayfront Park. And for active runners, there are many marathons and charity events in which you can participate.

Tennis lovers should visit the island of Key Biscayne. This island is well known in the tennis community for its annual tennis tournament, in which Serena Williams and Roger Federer participated in recent years.

In the West Palm Beach area, golfers will feel right at home. Some well-known and highly prized golf tournaments take place there and attract many golf celebrities every year.

In addition to that, the southern part of Florida is known worldwide for its excellent boating opportunities and yacht construction. Events such as boat shows and exhibitions each year in Miami and Fort Lauderdale attract hundreds of thousands of visitors.

South Florida is very interesting for international boaters and has an excellent reputation for its marinas and houses with private boat docks.

The two major cities in the state, Miami and Fort Lauderdale, have cruise ports from which the cruise ships start their journeys into the Caribbean and Latin and Central America.

When you take a cruise, you have the option of a multiday cruise or a short cruise. The short or one-day cruises are usually to the Bahamas or sometimes to a casino ship on the ocean.

If you do not like the casino ship, then you can also choose to go to a casino on dry land. There are several casinos in the metro area of Miami/Fort Lauderdale that offer a great chance to win the jackpot. Even when you are not a gambler, a visit to a casino is always recommended because they offer a lot of other entertainments. Well-known artists and singers perform in the casinos, and you will find many good restaurants, bars, and bistros in the complex as well. A good example is the Hard Rock Hotel in Hollywood, Florida.

Another important point is the big gay scene that calls South Florida home. This scene is like the icing on the cake of colorful cultures mixed together, and it is another interesting facet of the Florida lifestyle.

What Does Florida Offer to Business Owners?

The state of Florida is working very hard to expand opportunities for new businesses and new companies because it wants to reduce its dependence on its two main industries: tourism and real estate. The efforts open up new possibilities for business investors and startups.

Welcome economic activities include IT, international trade, research, and health care. Florida is an excellent location for the international trade because of its geographical position. The ports and airports in Miami and Fort Lauderdale are expanded and under transformation to become the main transportation and trade hubs to South America and overseas.

Starting a business or branch office is relatively easy to do in Florida, and the subsequent costs and taxes are very attractive in comparison to some other locations in the world. With competent partners, the necessary activities can be arranged quickly and successfully.

To open a company, you must have a United States visa. The various visa options that are available to you cannot be discussed in this book. For questions and requests, we can certainly provide the right support and the best connections.

A successful business or a correspondingly high investment gives you the chance to get a green card. The advantage of a green card is it allows you to stay in the United States to pursue your business transactions and enjoy your life's dream.

Explore your opportunities in Florida and put your plans and visions into reality with competent experts and professionals. This goal is much easier to achieve when you already have a foothold in this location.

Such a first foothold can be a property. You can discuss your questions for your individual business project locally with competent specialists. Your challenges will be cleared and dissolved easier when you reside locally. Also, a house is a solid investment that can be used for your business venture as collateral.

What Does Your Dream Home Look Like?

One of the most important sectors of the economy in Florida is real estate. We have beautiful properties of all sizes and all possible levels of amenities—with and without a pool; with and without a dock; detached house, townhouse, or condominium. Are you looking for beachfront at the complex? Views to the ocean, a boat channel, or a garden view? With a surrounding yard or without?

Do you think these are tough questions? Not necessarily. The term property is the same in all countries. It is a fixed, enclosed living quarter on a piece of land.

Such a building has massive constructed exterior walls, doors, and windows, a floor, and a roof. Such a property provides shelter against wind and weather and protects against threats from the outside world. In this retreat, you can withdraw, recharge our batteries, relax, and get ready for the next challenge or the next life adventure in Florida.

Everyone defines his or her requirements for such a retreat differently and in his or her own way. You certainly have different requirements than I have. To find what you are looking for and what is important to you, it is necessary to know what benefits each type of property offers. Your main requirements and wishes determine the selection of your possible dream homes, and then you choose the best home for you.

Now you are surely interested in what types of property are available in Florida and how to choose from these. Let us start with the real estate education.

There are existing homes and new construction, or homes

that are not built yet. The existing homes are either solid-built houses, prefabricated houses, or trailer homes, and they have at least one previous owner. These homes are offered as a resale on the market. Some houses are renovated and ready to move in, while others need some renovations and upgrades.

New construction homes are sold directly from the construction company and are solid-constructed houses under the applicable building code of Florida. You are the first owner of such a home.

There are detached homes and townhouses with different lot sizes and condominiums. The property can be located in an enclosed community that is protected by a fence and a gate or without any security enclosure. Some communities also provide community facilities such as a community pool, exercise room, and a clubhouse.

If you enjoy boating, you will be certainly interested in a private dock so that your yacht can be parked at your dock in your own backyard.

Let us unravel this big mishmash and compare the advantages and details of each property type.

Before we go into the details, let me clear up some prejudices that are often widespread, especially in the media. Surely you have seen headlines like this: HOUSES IN FLORIDA FLYING THROUGH THE AIR, NO SOLID CONSTRUCTION, and much more. This is simply not true.

These messages are simply sensational journalism. A headline with flying houses always sells better than a good, researched report about storm preparedness and help provided by the neighboring community during and after the storm.

Yes, sometimes there are flying roofs or parts of them in the air, but these are generally houses that are older and that no longer meet applicable Florida building codes.

Or it might be a trailer home whose design does not meet the building regulations or is not properly anchored to the ground, or the owner neglected maintenance on his or her trailer home.

Let us be honest, you certainly know that severe weather and natural disasters occur everywhere, even in your own country. At home, you also have such climatic conditions too, and you also may see flying roofs, even when the house is solidly constructed. The resulting damage is similar.

Let us take a quick look at the buildings in Florida only to get an idea. Information about construction details and statements regarding stability and durability, as well as the latest building codes, should be discussed with a home or building inspector when you are in the purchase process.

Older houses were often built as a frame construction. That means that on a foundation slab, the exterior walls were built as a frame structure, including roof, and connected to the base slab.

This frame structure is covered on both sides with wood. The existing cavities between the outer timber wall and the inner timber wall are filled with insulation and the necessary supply lines like water pipes and electricity lines.

This construction methode was replaced in the 1950s by concrete block construction, but there are still some isolated properties left that are built this old construction method.

In concrete block construction, the exterior walls are constructed with blocks, while on the inside the walls are covered with drywall sheets or plaster. The supply lines like electricity lines or water pipes, are not always beneath the drywall or plaster. The roof is made of wood, and its load is mostly carried by the outer walls. The roof is connected with the exterior walls using metal straps.

The interior is usually done using a wooden or steel structure, which is covered on both sides with drywall. Interior walls are usually not load bearing, and therefore the interior structure is very flexible.

Hurricane Andrew in 1992 gave rise to many building regulations, which have been continuously adapted since that time and are focused on the climatic conditions and requirements. These building regulations are binding and apply to any new construction buildings and to any modernization or renovation of older buildings.

As a result of the climatic challenges, the building code has also changed the construction methods for new homes. Many new buildings are manufactured from cast concrete. In this case, a steel strut design is built on the foundation slab and boards are screwed on both sides of the steel struts. Then this steel structure is filled with concrete. Once the concrete has cured, the boards are removed and the roof is placed on the exterior walls. Window and door openings are spared in the concrete casting. The hurricane-safe impact glass windows and doors are put into the spared openings.

The last steps of the interior work are done in the usual way. Building codes must be followed for water supply, electricity supply, and internal insulation.

Following the existing building codes is mandatory for new constructed buildings, while in the modernizing of older homes a modified version of building codes is used. The appropriate building department in each city is the best information resource to find the applicable building codes regulations.

Why Do Property Sizes Differ from Those in Other Countries?

The United States calculates distance in inch, foot, yard, and acre, while other countries use centimeters, meters, square meters, and hectares. These lengths and surface measurements must be converted accordingly.

To make it simple and to get a rough idea of size, the ratio of 1:10 is recommended. If a house has a size of 1500 square feet, then it corresponds to roughly 150 square meters.

For the conversion, you can use the following information:

1 inch = 2.54 cm

12 inches = 1 foot (12 x 2.5 cm = 30.48 cm)

3.28 feet = 1 meter

1 square foot = 1 foot x 1 foot

1 yard = 3 feet

1 acre = 43,560 square feet

This should help you to generally understand property details more easily and visualize the measurements. When you get the property information already converted, you can check and verify the facts.

How Do You Understand Street Names in Florida?

The vast majority of cities, not just in Florida but in the United States as a whole, are planned. This means towns and villages are not grown wild, but they were created and planned on the drawing board.

This makes it very easy to get around in any unfamiliar city. There are so-called avenues and streets. Other names such as boulevard, way, court, place, and square we will skip here, because only the principle shall be explained for better orientation.

Avenues run in a south to north direction, while streets run in an east to west direction. Residential areas are exclusively for single-family homes and multifamily houses that are rented. Rental apartment buildings are generally built closer to access roads in the residential area, while single-family homes are built behind rental apartment buildings.

Within residential areas, no commercial buildings, such as shops, gas stations, banks, and cinemas are allowed. One exception to this is fire stations. They are placed every two to three kilometers, and water hydrants are places almost at every third house for their water supply. In case of a fire, a quick fire extinction is guaranteed.

Additionally, these hydrants and the close distance to fire stations have a positive impact on your homeowner's insurance and you get a discount from your insurance company.

What Kinds of Properties Are Available?

Properties differ in terms of design, lot size, and type of management. There are detached and connected buildings. The connected houses can be differentiated into duplexes, townhouses, multiplexes.

At some properties, the homeowner determines everything, from exterior design to landscaping and painting. With other properties, there is a homeowner's association with established rules and regulations that the homeowner must follow. These regulations often determine the appearance of the property's exterior and the landscaping.

In some of these communities, approval of the homeowner's association board is necessary when buyers purchase a property. This is normally only a formality, but it has to be taken into consideration, because it impacts the transaction. The rules and regulations of a homeowner's association should be provided by the seller as soon as the sale transaction has started and the offer is made. You will find more details about homeowner's association boards later in this book.

Original Florida Style.

What Is a Detached Property in Florida?

The most popular type of property is the family home. Such a house has no direct connection with other houses and sits on a piece of land. Residential property lots are relatively large in comparison to those in other countries. For example, in my neighborhood, the lot size is at least 8,000 square feet (equivalent to 800 square meters), and my own site is actually 10,500 square feet (1050 square meters).

In new construction areas, such large lot sizes are relatively rare. The usual lot sizes in these communities are comparable to those in Europe and other countries.

On your property showing tour, you will notice that some

homes are elevated and look as if they are built on a hill. You might think that is for flood protection and that you are in a flood zone. However, the actual reason is the stony and extremely hard ground, which makes the excavation of a pit for the supply lines—water and sewer—very difficult and expensive. As a solution to this problem, a hill is heaped and the necessary supply lines are laid into the hill underneath the house's foundation slab.

As already mentioned, Florida is flat, and that is especially true at the southern tip of the state. Much of the state was formerly swampland, as you still find it in the Everglades. The swamps are a consequence of the high water table, and development on former swamp ground is only possible after the proper drainage of the ground.

Beneath the thin layer of alluvial dirt is shell limestone, and this ground layer makes the excavation of pits for foundations a problem. The hard shell of limestone is also the reason that you will not find cellars or basements under the buildings in Florida.

To my knowledge, there is only one existing house with a basement in Fort Lauderdale. Another basement can be found in the Deering Estate at Cutler Bay. However, that house once belonged to the industrial magnate Charles Deering, who had enough money for the construction of a basement. Today, the Deering Estate is a museum, and visitors can explore this basement on their tour.

There are many different styles of houses available in Florida, and you will certainly find the right one for you. For the nostalgic person, there is the Old Florida Style. These are one-story, single-family homes with a smaller footprint.

Many of these houses have wall or window units rather than a central air-conditioning system, because the roofs are flat with a little roof slope. As a result of this little slope, there is not sufficient space available to put in the ductwork necessary for a central air-conditioning system.

The entire living area of such a house is on the ground floor. These houses usually have two or three bedrooms and one or two bathrooms. The kitchen and living room, as well as additional areas such as laundry room and sun room (in Europe these enclosures are called wintergardens), are not used as a criteria for the size of house, but they are included in the total living area.

Older homes often have a carport rather than a garage. Sometimes carports and garages are converted into living space in later alterations. In this case, the house has an additional bedroom but no garage. The property information often shows the original property design.

In the case of multistory houses, the public home space such as kitchen and living room are on the ground floor, while the bedrooms and bathrooms for family members are located upstairs.

The floors are connected by staircases in various designs. Elevators in private homes are reserved for only very high-priced properties.

Detached houses, especially older homes in established neighborhoods, usually have no mandatory homeowner communities. That means there are no regulations over what homeowners can do with their property when making changes like paint color and landscaping. They also do not have to pay monthly fees for maintenance. The homeowner is his or her own boss.

Townhouses in a community.

What Is a Townhouse in Florida?

Surely you know the term attached houses from your home country. This form of house is available in the United States too. However, there are some differences to learn, and the meaning of attached house in your home country may be slightly different from that in the United States and Florida.

In Florida, we call these homes townhouses and villas. A townhouse is usually a multistory building, meaning it has at least two floors. The floors are connected with stairs. (Elevators are not common in such houses.)

Such townhouses generally have a garage on the ground floor. A carport is unusual. The garages in these houses are used not only for cars, but also as a utility room for washer and dryer as well as for the water heater and central air-conditioning system.

The second style of rowhouse is the villa. A villa in the United States is not comparable to the expression villa in Europe. In Europe, for example, the word villa means a large property on an oversized lot. In the United States, on the other hand, a villa is a single-story attached house with a relatively small lot.

The room count of such a house is usually two to three bedrooms and two bathrooms. Due to its construction, a villa usually has no garage and only one or two parking spaces for cars in front of the house.

The lots of rowhouses or townhouses are smaller than those of detached houses. The usual lot size is between one thousand to three thousand square feet (about one hundred to three hundred square meters).

Due to the construction style of townhouses or rowhouses, these properties are usually part of a community with a homeowner's association. These communities have community rules and regulations. Details on this topic can be found in a later chapter.

Detached single-family home in a community.

What Is a Condominium (or Condo) in Florida?

You are certainly familiar with apartments that you can buy, own, and occupy yourself from your home country. In the United States, such a property is called a condominium, or condo.

The common room count of condominiums is one or two bedrooms and one or two bathrooms. One bathrooms is usually a full bathroom with a bathtub or a stall shower, and the second one is either a half bath or a second full bath. A half bathroom has only a toilet and a vanity.

A condominium is located in a multistory building. Each condominium unit is owned by an individual owner. Each apartment is limited to the four surrounding walls of condominium. Every part of the structure that is outside of the unit walls is owned by all condominium owners together. These building parts include all inside and outside amenities—hallways, lobby, pool, elevator, exercise rooms, etc.—of the condominium complex.

There are two types of condominium buildings, and the difference between them is the building design. Condominium buildings with no more than four floors are called garden apartments. It depends on the number of floors and the type of residents—for example, seniors in a 55+ community—if there is a common elevator in such a building. As a little hint, you can keep in mind that buildings with only two floors rarely have an elevator.

All condominium buildings with more than four floors have an elevator. Such buildings are called high-rises.

The common area and amenities in a condominium complex include trash chutes, elevators, laundry rooms, pool, garden areas, garages, and all areas that are beyond the walls of the individual unit. These building elements and areas are maintained by the entire condominium community. To fund this maintenance, each individual condo owner has to pay a monthly maintenance fee.

For the administration of condominiums, there are two options. One option is explained above, the second option is a co-op, short for cooperative. In a co-op, all condominiums and all other common property elements belong to all owners together. Each owner only gets a share of the cooperative equity. This kind of property ownership may not exist in your home country.

In a coop, the financing options for a buyer are very limited or nonexistent, because the apartments in such a complex are not in the individual ownership of the occupant and therefore cannot be used as loan security or collateral. The buyers or condominium occupants are only shareholders.

If you are interested in buying a coop condominium, you should definitely check into how the condominium complex is administered, because maintenance costs and the ownership of the units are different and might have legal consequences.

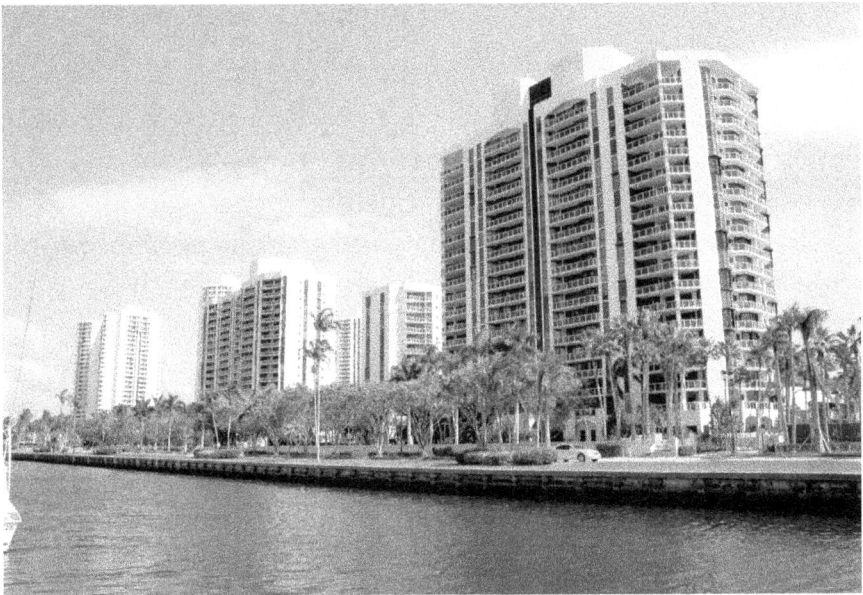

Condominium in a high-rise.

What Are the Advantages and Disadvantages of the Various Real Estate Types?

Real estate properties in Florida are diverse and have many advantages and challenges. As a potential buyer, you should take all of them into consideration.

To find the best matching dream property for you, it is important that you know what your goal is when buying a house or a condominium.

Do you want to use the property only for yourself and your family, or do you want to rent it out temporarily or all year round?

Is the house or condo only a short-term investment that you will purchase with the intention to make a quick gain and sell it again?

If you want to use the property only for yourself and your family, you should focus more on the location and the interior equipment and not on the price. Good, solid construction and an appealing surrounding neighborhood should have a big impact on your decision so that your dream home appreciates over the time of your ownership and that you can sell it later with a gain.

It is also important whether you plan to constantly reside in your new home or only for a few months each year. When you own a single-family home with a surrounding yard, please keep in mind that the yard needs to be maintained during your absence. In this case, you will need a professional service that takes care of the lawn mowing and the trimming of trees and shrubs. Otherwise you might get a violation notice from the city when your lawn and landscaping is overgrown.

Whether you rent out your property temporarily or all year long, you will need a professional manager. He or she will take the necessary actions on your behalf. Even if your tenant is obligated, based on the rental agreement, to mow the lawn, there are many other obligations that cannot be completed by your tenant. A good example is the collection of monthly rent payments and initiating and monitoring of repairs. Such tasks are only allowed for real estate professionals or homeowners.

Such duties require a real estate license; your best friend or your neighbor is not entitled to do that for you, because that would be illegal. You'll find more information on this in a later chapter – What Are the Professional Requirements.

If your property is located in a homeowner or condominium owner community, there are a few more details to consider in case you intend to rent your house or your condominium.

The administration of the individual ownership—that is, your single-family home or your condominium—is separate from the administration of the common areas, the common buildings and the exterior and grounds. The administration of the grounds and buildings are done by the management company of the homeowner's association; the management of an individual property is not one of their tasks and needs to be organized by you as the property owner.

The duties of a homeowner's association manager and the maintenance of the common areas in the home or condo community are based on the rules and regulations of the community. These rules and regulations are binding for every owner in the community, and when you buy such a property you must accept them.

These rules and regulations, for example, state who is responsible for the exterior of the building, the landscaping, the roads, the pool, the exercise room, etc., and how much each and every home or condominium owner has to pay every month for maintenance. These tasks are performed by the hired management company.

When you want to rent your property in such a community (house or condominium), the management company for the common area is only partly involved. This company does not work for the individual owners and will not perform any duties like collection of rent payments, management of the rental proceedings (including marketing), initiating repairs, or maintaining the unit. The monthly rent or payments for utilities like water and electricity are not this company's focus. As the unit owner, you have to take care of these things.

However, the home or condominium owner board has the right to approve the length of a lease contract, the frequency of leases, and the tenant. With this approval, the board will make sure that the rights of the other owners are not violated or limited and that the tenant understands the community rules and regulations.

The rights of the home or condominium owner association is defined in the community documents, and each home or condominium owner is given a copy when purchasing a property. One of the rules is, for example, the limitation of the maximum number of tenants or the maximum number of leases during a year, so that the units cannot be used like a hotel. Furthermore, there is a mandatory financial and criminal background check for each buyer or tenant. Such an examination of the buyer's or tenant's financial and criminal background is not common in every country. In Europe, this process is generally limited to the credit score and government databases.

If the background check shows no irregularities, then the buyer or tenant is invited to an interview with several owners' representatives. They want to know their new neighbors and want to familiarize them with the regulations and the community rules.

Background checks are conducted for the protection of the entire community. Each person who is living in the community should feel safe. This background check can only be done within the strict limitations of the Fair Housing Act of the United States, a federal law that is applied in all states in the same way; the infringement of this law is a violation of a national law and will be prosecuted by the Federal Department of Housing and Urban Development of the United States.

What Does *Fair Housing* Mean?

This is a fixed term and can be translated as antidiscrimination law. The United States has been a melting pot of nations for its entire history. As you know, Americans had some unpleasant episodes in their history, with the integration of other cultures, such as African Americans and Native Americans, and they have learned from these and adapted.

The Fair Housing Act states that no discrimination shall be made in the following areas: color, race, nationality, disability, religion, marital status, or sexual orientation. These regulations apply to all areas of life in the United States, but especially to real estate. Failure to comply with this law will result in legal consequences.

This law is also the reason why real estate professionals will not give you an answer to specific questions about neighborhood or local residents. Some questions that Realtors cannot answer include the following:

• Is this neighborhood safe?

• Is there crime in this neighborhood?

• How many [members of a certain race, creed, nationality, etc.] live there?

The property specialist will not provide the answers to these questions, but he or she will assist you in doing your own research by advising you to visit the sheriff's website or call the police to obtain information about this topic.

Is a Real Estate Property a Lucrative Investment for You?

Today, many are looking for a new business idea to make quick and easy money. But honestly, do you really think that money is falling like bread out of the sky and you only have to pick it up?

If you want to earn money, you must work for it. That has been so since the beginning of life and will stay that way at least for the near future. When you want to bake bread and need flour, you must spread the seeds in the spring and protect the delicate plants from germination to maturity, cherish and maintain them, water and weed and expel the birds; otherwise, there will be no bread.

It is the same when you want to earn income with real estate properties. Depending on how much money you want to earn and in what time, the real estate market in Florida is a great place to start. This market offers something for everybody.

Using our example from the seeds to the bread for the real estate market, it means you purchase a single-family home or condominium at a low price. Then you renovate or remodel the property and put it back on the market right away with a higher price. Or you rent the property and collect income for a few months or years, selling it later when the property has appreciated. Either way, you will win.

You might be asking, what is a low price? That depends on the location of the real estate property and your expectation for the gain of the investment. There are some locations where you pay as much for a small one-bedroom/one-bathroom condominium as you might pay for a single-family house at a different location. And you may be able to get a higher percentage gain for that one-bedroom apartment after renovation than with a house. Your gain depends on the quality of the renovation, the location of the property, and the local real estate market.

There are thousands of very lucrative real estate properties in the Florida market that will meet your wishes and your expectations. You only have to make a smart choice. These real estate purchases are as secure as in your home country—maybe even more secure, depending on your home country. In the United States, you are, even as a foreign national, the owner of the house or the condominium, with all rights and obligations. That is not the case in all countries of the world.

However, the do-it-yourself method of property deals in a

foreign country is not recommended because the real estate property transfer is handled differently than in your home country. In many countries, you need a special attorney to execute such deals.

You also have to keep in mind that a real estate professional from your home country will not be able to help you. He or she will not satisfy the legal requirements for the real estate business in the United States, will not have the knowledge, and will not be able to get the necessary data and information about the properties.

This is the case not only in Florida or even in the United States, but in every other country. Each country has its own real estate laws and regulations that you have to respect; otherwise you will not get what you want.

Here is a sample calculation for an investment property (fictive data):

Apartment property with four units,
Monthly rent: $800.00 per unit

Cash purchase price: $200,000.00
(a mortgage is not taken into account)

Rental income (4 x $800.00)	$38,400.00
vacancy 10%	$3,840.00
Gross income	$34,560.00
Costs (estimated 40%) Repair, insurance, taxes etc.	$13,824.00
Operational Income	$20,736.00
Depreciation (for rental units annual linear 27.5 years according to the tax regulations)	-$7,272.73
Income before taxes (seek advice from an accountant for the necessary relevant tax details and calculations)	$13,463.27

How Can You Fulfill Your Dream of Owning a Property in Florida?

Perhaps you already own a property in your home country and think to yourself, I know everything. What new knowledge can this book provide me? If I want to buy a house, I will go by myself and look what is available on the market. When I find something I like, I'll call any agent broker or I'll call the agent who has his or her sign on the property or in the window of the house.

Yes, you are right. You can do it that way, because that is what you know from your home country. However, each country has different rules and business habits. Even in the

European Union, each member country has its own regulations and laws. Therefore, it is a mistake to stick to that knowledge, because it is no longer valid when you cross the border.

And if you look further into the distance, it becomes more and more complicated. No matter where in the world you are going to purchase a property, the do-it-yourself method is the most expensive, the most dangerous, and the worst you can chose.

There's more. You might think you have bought a house, but the contract in the foreign language says something completely different. To get your legal rights, you have to go to court in that foreign country and that can be very expensive. Hiring a local real estate specialist is a better and safer option and will cost you nothing in Florida because the seller pays the commission and your agent gets his or her fair share of the commission.

In other countries, it may be the case that you think you have purchased and paid for a property and after the fact you find out that you are unfortunately out of luck. It could be, for example, that you as a foreign national are not allowed to buy land or a property because the national laws prohibit property ownership for foreign nationals. In this case, you spent a lot of money and did not get anything in return. To get your money back, you have to go to court.

The United States is not one of those countries. Here, you are the owner, with all rights and obligations. However, it is not recommended to purchase any real estate property in Florida on your own.

You certainly wonder why. There are so many real estate

websites on this topic, and they offer all types of real estate. Compared to those in Europe and other foreign countries, the property prices are inexpensive, the location and the neighborhoods look clean and well-maintained, and you can financially afford the real estate dream.

But—and this is the most important point—the real estate purchase process is handled completely differently from your home country. The tasks and duties of a real estate agent in your home country are not comparable to those of a real estate agent or broker in Florida. Special attorneys who prepare real estate contracts are common in European countries, and maybe in your home country too—these are not common here.

Contracts in Florida are prepared as standard contracts by the Florida Realtors' and Florida Attorneys' Associations and these contracts are used by the real estate professionals in real estate transactions. These standard contracts are extremely safe and easy to handle and do not need the service of an attorney to be a legally binding document.

Let us come back for a moment to the real estate websites on the Internet. They are all so beautiful and colorful. They will show you everything in dazzling colors and details, but often the presented information about the property is incomplete, incorrect, or outdated. An update of the property data is rarely done automatically and must be performed manually by the data owner. These updates are often forgotten, and the data stay there forever.

The only correct information and current data you can obtain in the United States—and in our case, in Florida—comes from a licensed real estate professional.

Real estate specialists in Florida belong to the various local real estate associations, and based on their membership they have an excellent data pool available for you that you cannot access on your own with the real estate portals. Each local real estate specialist pays annual association dues in order to gain access to this data and information that are not available to the public.

It is therefore in your own interest as a buyer to hire a locally active real estate expert. No broker in your home country, no friend from another city or another state in the United States can offer you the service that you need for the project of your residence in paradise.

You can only obtain this service, which will save you a lot of money, from a local real estate specialist in Florida. And this service is only available when you hire a local real estate specialist in Florida.

Is a Visa Necessary to Purchase a Property?

That depends on what you are planning to do with your dream home and how long you intend to stay in the United States and Florida.

The United States has what is called the Visa Waiver Agreement with thirty-eight nations worldwide. That means that the citizens of these thirty-eight countries are allowed to enter the United States with their passports, and they are permitted to stay for ninety days, but they are not permitted to work.

If you want to stay for a longer period of time than ninety

days or you are not on the list of the thirty-eight nations, then you have to apply for a visa at the closest embassy or consulate of your home country. You will have to contact them first to find out where to go and what to bring with you.

A tourist and business visa for six months is a great way to stay legally and temporarily in the United States. With this visa, you obtain a residence permit for 180 days a year. However, with this visa you are not permitted to accept a job and work in the United States. There are a few exceptions to this rule, but be very careful and ask an immigration attorney for advice.

This is only a short discussion of this topic; there are more visa options available that may fit better for your intentions. Laws and regulations surrounding US visas are too complex to cover here in great detail. When you need more information, send us an e-mail and we will assist you in finding the right attorney. You find the e-mail address at the end of this book.

Back to the question above: the simple answer is that for the purchase of a dream home in Florida, you do not need a visa as long as you are from one of the thirty-eight waiver visa countries.

What Is Different About Purchasing Real Estate in Florida Versus in Your Home Country?

To get to this point, it is necessary that you think about your own country and how the real estate professionals work there. Because I do not know where you are from, I will use the example of a property purchased in Germany. Please compare on your own how your country fits into this process.

Usually, the real estate buyer or tenant starts his or her search in the local newspapers, looking in the classified advertisements for interesting and matching properties. When buyers or tenants do not find anything that they like in the printed newspaper, they search the Internet via several available real estate portals.

For example, when tenants are looking for an apartment with three rooms, kitchen, and bathroom for 1,000 euro rent, they will certainly find something. In these online portals, everyone—property owner or agent—can market their apartments and homes either free of charge or for a flat fee, and they hope that many potential buyers or tenants read this advertisement.

These published advertisements, however, are only a limited selection of properties. The published properties are offered by the owners. Brokers or agents only put properties on these portals when the seller reimburse them or when they expect better market success with the active promotion of the property in the media.

Advertisements on online real estate portals with many readers are not free of charge, and the period for ads are limited to one edition or a month. If the property is not under contract after that time period, the next advertisement fee is due. Not every property owner is willing to pay for such a marketing and they stay away from these platforms and that limits the available number of properties very much.

The purpose of such advertisements is not necessarily to promote the specific property for sale or rent, but rather to motivate buyers or tenants to call the real estate office in the advertisements. With the call, the agent has the chance to get a home buyer or tenant as a customer and will offer them the real estate services of the office. The agent will mostly show properties in the office portfolio and will get a commission of 6 percent plus VAT from the buyer when the sale contract closes. If you hire the agent, you are responsible for the commission payment.

If you are looking in the property market in Germany for a rental apartment as a tenant, you are responsible for paying the broker's commission once you have chosen one of the offered and shown rental units and signed the lease contract. The brokerage fee is calculated on the monthly rent of the property, and in Germany this fee must not exceed two months' rent payments.

In Germany, it is common for the buyer or tenant to pay a commission to his or her agent or broker for the services. The services that you receive as a buyer or a tenant are much more limited than in the United States. (Remember, your country may have different rules for who pays for real estate services.)

Please be aware that real estate portals in Germany are not well maintained and have no automatic data update or deletion; there may be some properties listed that have already been sold or rented. Also the real estate listings on the portals are not exclusively represented by the advertising office, but by everybody else who is in the business. The reason for these advertisements is to attract customers who are willing and motivated to buy or to rent and not to market and promote the listed property.

It can happen that the listed property stays on the portals because the advertising period is not yet expired or the advertiser has no intention to delete it because customers are still calling.

Property details are not always up-to-date and accurate on the portals because these ads have to be maintained manually, and not every real estate professional takes the time and care to keep their ads updated and correct.

Therefore these portals are not very reliable in regards to the content.

These examples show that ads about available properties are highly dependent on the advertiser's intention and the monthly ad budget, which is planned for the individual property.

For this reason, only a small portion of all available properties on the market have the latest and correct information and are shown on real estate websites.

The above statement is based on my own experience and research on the Internet. The agents who marketed and tried to sell my own properties in Germany did not listen to my updates. I kept them informed about price changes and more details on the properties, but they did not make changes in their advertisements or their flyers, and neither did they bring me a buyer.

This is the same on all real estate portals, because there is no regulation and control over who is allowed to advertise and what to advertise.

Does your home country have different regulations? How do real estate professionals work in your country?

When you see properties from the United States advertised on the Internet portals in foreign countries, the advertiser has often requested these properties as show objects, or sometimes they have been stolen from United States websites to attract leads from potential customers. The intention is to sell these leads to agents in the United States or to lead generating companys for money.

When you call the advertiser to get more information about that specific dream home, you will often learn that the property has already sold or is under contract, and the advertiser "forgot" to delete the ad (because he or she wants to get further leads from it).

To make sure that you get the property you want, you have to contact and hire a local real estate specialist in the country where you intent to buy the property. Otherwise, you will not be successful in obtaining your dream home.

The market in the United States moves quickly and has a different dynamic than that in Europe or in other countries. The real estate property market here is much better organized and represented on the Internet, for example. You will find a much bigger selection of available properties. The above-mentioned problem with the property data is much less likely to occur.

There is another very important legal difference between a German and a Florida real estate professional. A German real estate professional can open up his or her business tomorrow. The only requirement is to go to the local registry and get a business license. It is not necessary to provide qualification papers and the relevant knowledge and experience for this business activities.

In the United States, one must comply with various legal requirements to pursue the profession of real estate professional.

How is the real estate profession regulated in your country? Does this profession need a license and education? Please do not transfer your real estate knowledge from your home country to the real estate professionals in Florida. There are many differences.

What Are the Professional Requirements for a Real Estate Agent or Broker?

The job description and activity scope of real estate specialists are regulated and completely differently organized in the United States than in many other countries. A comparison list at the end of this description shows the most important differences between Florida and Germany.

Adapt this list to your home country to figure out what differences exist in your case.

In order to enter the profession of real estate agent or broker in the United States, one must study this sector of the economy in English, because one must be familiar with the necessary business knowledge.

Once study is completed, admission to the state examination can be requested. This approval process for a future real estate agent includes the delivery of fingerprints and a personal background check. A punishment for drunk driving or any other criminal issues can mean the end for the new professional in the real estate industry.

The background check in Germany is a state certificate of good conduct. Please check for yourself if that is also necessary in your country when doing business as a real estate agent.

Once a background check is successfully completed, the agent will take the state exam. This exam is very challenging and includes not only work-related issues but also relevant information about tax laws, contract law, and possible financing options. The scope is limited to the basic understanding of the topics, and a future agent is encouraged to recommend that their customers seek the advice of a professional in other areas like accountants, lawyers, and loan officers for their individual situation and circumstances.

The real estate agent has to pass the state exam. About 80 percent of the students fail the exam, and they have only one more chance to pass before they have to start from square one again.

When the real estate professional has passed the state exam, he or she is issued a professional license from the office of the governor of Florida. The governor is the highest political office on the state level and is comparable to president of a federal state in Germany. In your country, it might be a different issuing administration for business licenses.

Real estate licenses are valid for two years and must be renewed after that time. Such a renewal will only be approved when the agent fulfills the continuing education requirements and proves that to the state. If the requirements are not completed, the license is void, and practicing the real estate profession without a license is illegal and will be punished.

What Does Sale Agent/Associate Mean?

During the first two years of practice, the sale agent/associate (that is the official name for a real estate professional) works under the supervision of a broker. The agent is an independent contractor in that brokerage firm. That means the agent is not an employee and receives no salary.

During this time, the sale associate has to take further classes to deepen his or her business knowledge. The attendance at these classes needs to be proven to the licensing administration.

If the sale agent does not comply with these legal requirements, he or she will lose the license and will no longer be permitted to work as an agent in the real estate business. If the agent continues to work in the real estate field, he or she will be in violation of the law and risks being punished.

For you as the real estate buyer, it is very important that you request that an agent show you his or her valid real estate license. That is the only protection for you that the agent knows how to handle a real estate transaction and that this agent has a broker who supervises the agent.

What Tasks Does the Sale Agent Perform for You?

Your sale agent is your trusted representative in your real estate purchase transaction. He or she will guide you through the entire sales process and tell you which individual steps need to be done, when they need to be done, and how to complete them. He or she will also assist you in obtaining and submitting the necessary documents for each step and will let you know when each step must be started and completed based on the purchase contract time line so that the transaction will be successful.

A real estate professional will help you get into your new dream home in Florida quickly and happily.

Do You Have to Pay for your Agent's Services?

The services of a sale agent do not cost you anything out of your own pocket. Based on the legal regulations in the United States and in Florida, the property owner/seller pays the commission, and the commission is part of the seller's transaction costs. The total amount of the commission is divided between the two agents, listing agent and sale agent.

For more details, please read the chapter on the closing statement of your real estate transaction.

Why Shouldn't You Use the Listing Agent as Your Sale Agent?

You can certainly call the listing agent, but you will give away the best card that you have in this transaction, and you will make the real estate transaction much more complicated for yourself, the seller, and the agent. You do not save anything when using the listing agent, because you do not pay your sale agent. The seller of the property will pay your agent at the closing of the transaction.

There are a few very important reasons why you should not call or use the listing agent in a real estate transaction:

1. The listing agent has a so-called listing contract with the seller of the property. In this contract, the listing agent agrees with the seller what the seller expects from the listing agent and how the property should be marketed during the listing period.

2. The seller and the listing agent also agree on the commission amount. This agreement states exactly how much money the seller will pay for the service of selling the property at the closing of the sale transaction.

3. You should know that with the signing of the listing agreement, the listing agent and the seller establish a confidential relationship. That means that the listing agent is the trusted representative of the seller and will always act in the best interest of the seller—his or her boss. The listing agent is not allowed to build a trust relationship with you as the buyer, and your best interest is not the listing agent's focus.

One of these confidential or best interests of the seller is the lowest sale price the seller is willing to accept. As a buyer, you are keenly interested in this information, because it gives you the opportunity to make a correspondingly low bid. The listing agent knows the lowest price of the seller, but he or she is not allowed to share this information with you.

Also, the listing agent will not reveal to you confidential information relating to the condition of the property such as construction defects. The agent will only notify you of obvious defects and will recommend a home inspection to investigate the house condition and construction.

All information you give the listing agent, such as the price you are willing to pay, are not confidential, and this information will likely get back to the seller. Do you want to risk that and spoil your chance to buy your dream home?

I am sure you will agree that working with the listing agent is fighting a losing battle. Therefore, it is advisable for you to hire your own agent—your sale or buyer's agent.

In this case, the agent is your own trusted person to whom you disclose all your important details. The agent has to honor that trust. Should the agent not honor this confidential relationship, you have the option of proceeding legally and professionally against him or her. In serious offenses, you can file a claim for damages.

What Is a Buyer's Agreement?

To find the right real estate agent for you, you have to get together with your agent and find common ground. The agenda for this talk is that you and the real estate agent discuss what his or her duties and obligations are and what your rights and responsibilities are in the real estate transaction. You will only be successful when you both work together as a team.

During this meeting, the sale agent will present you a buyer's agreement and ask you to sign it. This document is a commitment that you as the buyer and he or she as the agent will work together in your real estate transaction.

With this agreement, the agent is obliged to maintain confidentiality, and he or she will only work in your best interest against the seller and the listing agent. At the same time, you promise to cooperate truthfully with your sale agent and provide him or her all documents and information necessary for the transaction.

The document also specifies what type of property you are looking for, for what purpose, how much you want to pay at maximum, how you want to pay, when you want to close on the property, and where you want to purchase the home.

This document is an additional protective mechanism for you. In case there are any irregularities, you have a document that is judicially enforceable.

As already mentioned, the agreed service in the buyer agreement is paid by the seller at the closing of the transaction; your benefit is that you have your own knowledgeable representative.

What Is a Realtor?

You have probably seen the term Realtor in many publications, and you may not know the meaning of that word. Realtor is a trademarked term and may only be used by real estate professionals who are members of the National Real Estate Association. The full name of the organization is National Association of Realtors (NAR), and its headquarters is in Chicago, Illinois.

The goal of this association is to establish professional standards in the real estate industry and to oversee them.

This association also represents the interests of real estate professionals and property owners nationwide and worldwide.

The so-called professional standards are put together in the Code of Ethics. This Code of Ethics sets the rules and regulations under which real estate professionals work together with you as a customer, with the public, and with other real estate professionals. These rules and regulations are amended annually according to the latest business practices and latest laws.

Each real estate professional who joins the National Association of Realtors is obliged to act in accordance with these rules and regulations. In return, the agents and brokers are allowed to carry the trademarked title Realtor.

On the other side, it also means that there real estate agents who are not members of the National Association of Realtors, and these are legally not allowed to use or carry the title Realtors. I will leave to your judgment whether or not these agents comply with the Code of Ethics.

To be on the safe side, it is recommended that you hire a Realtor over a non-Realtor, because the moral obligation to the business standards is stronger for Realtors.

REALTOR

What Do the Many Abbreviations on Business Cards of Some Real Estate Professionals Mean?

Once a real estate professional has successfully completed his or her state exam and has obtained a license, he or she is allowed to practice legally in the real estate business. The acquired knowledge in the real estate industry is the basic business, simple purchases and sales or rentals.

However, there are many additional education courses that are focused on specific parts of the real estate business. These additional studies have been created in cooperation with the National Association of Realtors, and they are open to any real estate professional. Realtors can decide whether they want to invest their own money and time into such additional training and broaden their expertise.

These additional courses do not count for the continuous education requirements of the state of Florida for the real estate license renewal. These courses are add-ons and show that the real estate professional is very engaged and interested in his or her profession.

The more education a real estate professional has, the more

knowledge and skills he or she brings to the table in order to make your purchase transaction successful and smooth.

Some examples for an international/global dedicated real estate professional are the designations and certifications CIPS, TRC, and RSPS. The specialized training ABR is not limited to international real estate transactions but focuses on real estate buyer demands, both nationally and internationally.

You will find the explanations for the abbreviations on the following pages.

CIPS
certified international property specialist

CIPS

The abbreviation CIPS means Certified International Property Specialist; it is a designation for the global business. This additional training focuses on international real estate transactions and specifics. The course is created by the National Association of Realtors.

Realtors with this education are trained in dealing with foreign real estate buyers and sellers. They know that in their customer's home country a property transaction is often done very differently than in the United States or Florida, and they explain these differences to their customers to protect them and to make them feel comfortable with the property transaction.

I can serve as a good example in this case. I started my career in the largest bank in Germany, in the real estate financing department. I combined my experience in financing with my knowledge of the real estate business in Florida. Today, I am the broker of my own international brokerage and I work with foreign buyers and sellers. In my case, Europe and the United States are perfectly linked to the benefit of both. I am also expending my expertise in this field to the Caribbean.

TRC

This second additional training is TRC, which means Transnational Referral Certification. The focus of this course is the transnational cooperation with other real estate professionals in the different countries worldwide.

This additional certification facilitates collaboration with a real estate professional from your home country on the basis of existing property laws in Florida and the United States and your country.

For example, if you have a broker or agent in your home country, he or she can work together with me when you give your approval. This cooperation is free of charge to you.

A referral commitment is signed between the two real estate professionals—your agent in your country and myself. This agreement regulates how and when the American Realtor may pay a referral fee to the foreign agent in your home country.

Such a compensation can be lucrative for the foreign agent and means only little or no effort for him or her. The agent in your home country only makes the connection between you and a local Florida broker. When the referral agreement is signed, the American real estate broker assumes all other activities and supports you as a customer in Florida.

For legal reasons, such a referral agreement can only be made between two real estate professionals. Referral arrangements with a private person and payments in real estate matters to private persons are illegal in the United States and Florida.

RSPS

Resort & Second-Home
Property Specialist

RSPS

A further additional training is the RSPS, or Resort and Second Home Property Specialist. Such a specialist is very familiar with the vacation homes and cottages in his or her given real estate market.

His or her focus is to assist you in a real estate transaction that focuses on lifestyle and vacation and your interests, such as golf, boating, diving, etc. Such specialists are familiar with your way of life and can help you to find exactly the right property for your lifestyle dream.

ABR

ABR stands for Accredited Buyer Representative. This agent represents mainly buyers in his or her transactions. Such an agent is specially trained in all concerns and requests of a real estate buyer. He or she works exclusively in your best interests as a buyer.

The buyer representative is your trusted person in the real estate transaction as a home buyer. With him or her, you can exchange confidential information without running the risk that the seller will receive this information and facts.

The task of your buyer's agent is to search for the right property for you from all the available properties, to show you the property, and to coordinate all activities required within the buying process until you close the transaction. The detailed steps and tasks are explained during the purchase transaction description in this book.

This is just a short list of the relevant additional training of a Florida real estate professional. This illustration is not complete, and additional educational opportunities for other real estate specialist areas exist, but they are not relevant to the subject of this book.

When you have your first meeting with your American real estate specialist, ask the agent to show you his or her additional education certificates and designations. The additional education courses are developed by the National Association of Realtors, and they are recognized in the real estate industry. The designations and certifications are seals of quality for your real estate specialist.

Why Might Some Agents Decide Not to Work with You?

I had the experience when I was not yet a broker that some real estate agents simply did not call me back or did not show me certain houses. This experience was frustrating and annoying, but there is an explanation for such behavior.

American real estate professionals are not permanently employed by their respective brokers. By that I mean that they do not receive a monthly salary. The agent is paid only when a real estate transaction closes and the property is sold.

That means that the agent only gets paid when you as the property buyer are able to pay for the property and close the deal.

The agent receives no reimbursement, for example, for gasoline used when driving around prospective buyers.

Another important bit of information is that the agent has to split his or her commission with his or her supervising broker. The splitting ratio between broker and agent varies from brokerage to brokerage.

Based on this presupposition, it makes no sense for real estate agents to provide you with their knowledge and expertise and show you several properties if you as a buyer are unable to complete the real estate transaction and pay the purchase price.

To find out if you are such a customer, agents might ask you to prove your financial capability for the purchase and discuss with you the financing options if your financial background is not strong enough for a cash purchase.

You certainly know such an approach from your home country. If you want to buy a property and you don't have sufficient cash funds at hand, you will have to go to your bank and get a credit approval before you can start any purchase activities and price negotiations.

Without this information, it doesn't make much sense for a real estate agent to go out with you on property hunt. Once you have found the right property, you must act immediately or the property will be snapped up by other interested parties before you even snap your fingers.

Often, there are multiple interested purchasers for a

property, and the buyer with the best arguments—cash or credit approval—will win the prize and purchase the home.

How Do You Find the Right Property Specialist?

It is like in every other service area. You speak with some real estate agents, and depending on which one seems to be the most competent and the most likeable to you, you start your real estate transaction with that person.

You can certainly ask a friend to recommend an agent, but keep in mind that your friend is not you. Your friend might have different objectives. Your friend, for example, might work very well with sale agent A, but this does not mean that you will also have a positive experience with agent A.

Please be careful with racing and rating lists, because they often do not reflect reality. The reviews in these portals are often courtesy reviews. The reviewer will be very cautious with his or her comments because he or she might be sued for speaking disparagingly.

I myself get several requests for recommendations and feedback every day. The requesters want to get a positive rating from me, although I have never worked with these people and therefore I cannot assess their knowledge, expertise, and skills.

Rely on your gut feeling and the proof of qualifications. Real estate professionals will gladly show you their credentials when they have nothing to hide. By the way, the following motto applies to this and any other business: class is better than mass.

That means that there are many real estate professionals in the market, but only a small group is excellent, educated, and experienced in the international real estate transaction business.

In case you have any questions in this regard, please feel free to e-mail me. You can find my e-mail address at the end of this book.

On the following page, you will find a list with some details about the work scope of real estate agents. You can use this list to compare agents in your home country with those in Florida.

	United States	Your Country
Who pays the agent/broker?	Seller	
What are the agent's duties?	Search the home, show it and guide buyer/seller through the transaction	
Who has the key for the home?	Each agent is able to get the key easily from the lockbox on the front door	
Who writes the contract?	The agent fills in the blanks in the standard contracts that are released by the state of Florida	
Is a license required?	Yes, an agent needs a license from the state	
Is continuing education required?	Yes, otherwise the license will not be renewed after two years	
How much is standard commission, and who pays it?	The common commission is 6 percent of the sale price; the seller pays	
Is there a professional regulation and control?	Yes, there is the Florida Real Estate Commission, which has control and punishment power outside the courts and is less expensive	

A Real Estate Transaction in the United States—Based on the Example of Florida

With the above information about the real estate industry in United States, we can turn to the next step: the search for your dream home and the successful purchase transaction of that home.

You are certainly excited to get your dream residence. It is important that you set your goal and your requirements for your residence in paradise in advance, before you start any activities. When you have gathered your ideas and requirements, you'll know what you expect from your real estate agent and how he or she can help you to achieve your goal.

The preparation and your knowledge will help you to find the right and matching real estate professional for you. You will realize very quickly when some detail or information that your agent tells you does not fit together.

It is also much easier to ask important questions and communicate your expectations and needs to the agent when you know exactly what you want from him or her.

Isn't that much more pleasant and safer for you than relying on the neighborhood and friend rumor mill?

Always remember: what has worked for your friend or neighbor might not work with your search for your dream home. Each dream house has its own surprises and secrets, and you and your agent have to discover them together and get them clarified.

Your real estate specialist will carefully explain to you the requirements for real estate transactions in the United States.

These transactions are often completely different from those in other countries around the world.

Your real estate agent in Florida has a longer task list to work on with you than an agent does in Europe. The agent is the main person in your real estate transaction. Together with him or her, you will get your dream home in the best possible location and at the best possible price.

Your real estate agent will present the complex buying process to you in an easy and understandable manner so that you will get your dream home quickly and without too much hassle. Only when you are a happy new homeowner your agent will be happy too, because he or she will get the commission.

Now, let us begin the search for Your Residence in Paradise!

Some Considerations Before You Start Your Property Search

If you have been to Florida, you already know a little bit about the area and its people. You have a feeling for what you like in this state and where you would like to live in your new home.

If you are a newcomer to Florida, ask yourself a few easy but important questions:

- When do you want to be in Florida, and how long do you want to stay?

- Do you want to have parties every day, or do you want to rest and relax?

- Are you a sport enthusiast, or are you a lazy bones with the intention to sunbathe all day long?

- Do you like boating, fishing, or diving?

- Is culture and entertainment in Florida very important to you, or do you prefer nature?

- How many rooms do you need in your home?

- What kinds of amenities are you looking for in your new home?

- How much do you want to spend for your new home?

- How much do you want to invest into your dream home?

- How do you want to pay for your dream home?

- Do you want to live in a community?

Make a checklist with the answers to these questions and bring this checklist with you when you meet your future real estate agent in Florida.

Determine Your Dream Home Location

If you are an adventurous person, for example, real estate locations south of Fort Lauderdale, toward Miami and Key West, might be right for you. In this area is the main center of tourism in southern Florida, and there are constant parties and events. The two major international airports in the region are Miami and Fort Lauderdale, and they are excellent starting points for your discovery trip to Florida.

Both cities also have large cruise ports, from which the cruise ships start their journeys into the Caribbean. In Fort Lauderdale, the airport and cruise port are within a one-mile radius.

Key West, the southernmost point of the continental United States, is another tourist attraction and is easily accessible by car or boat from Miami and Fort Lauderdale.

Key West has not only retained the charm of a former pirate's nest, but it is also an artists' colony, where Ernest Hemingway, Tennessee Williams, and Robert Frost lived and worked.

These locations have direct access to the open sea, and they are ideal locations for boat owners. Your boat can either be parked in the yard on a trailer or even better at your own private dock.

Access to the Atlantic Ocean is easy and quick in many residential areas via the many canals and the Intracoastal Waterway.

The Intracoastal is a natural channel that runs along the entire east coast, from Key West to Maryland. This waterway can be navigated even by sailing boats with tall masts, because drawbridges allow the boating in this waterway. It goes without saying that these locations are preferred and elegant residential areas.

The access to the Intracoastal Waterway is possible through the various inlets along the east coast. The inlets are natural entrance canals from the ocean into the Intracoastal Waterway. The inlets near Fort Lauderdale are the harbor entrance at cruise port in the south of Broward County and the Hillsboro Inlet in the north.

Because its residents come in large part from South America and Cuba, Miami is culturally influenced by the Latin-American and Spanish lifestyle. Fort Lauderdale, however, is more American in lifestyle, and Key West adds the Caribbean influence to this cultural mixture. This similar mixture exists on the southwest coast of Florida, but in a more tranquil atmosphere.

In Central Florida, you'll find Orlando, with its amusement parks including Walt Disney World, Universal Studios, and many others. Beaches and water sports, such as boating and fishing on the high seas, can be enjoyed from that location only after an hour's drive to the east or west coast.

Other interesting areas in this region include the vineyards and natural parks, as well as the NASA site, which includes the Kennedy Space Center.

As you move farther north, you will experience more and more the classic southern charm as seen in the movie Gone with the Wind and the flair of the Bible belt. The weather is more moderate. In the summer, temperatures are pleasant during the day, and in the winter, there may be one or another cold snap with scattered snowflakes and sometimes even a little bit of ice—so I have heard from friends who live in that area.

Cold waves in the winter are extremely rare in southern Florida and snowflakes do not exist, unless they are produced artificially at winter events in Miami and Fort Lauderdale.

If they occur at all, cold waves have a short duration, and the daytime temperatures are still pleasantly mild, similar to summer temperatures in northern Germany.

The summer temperatures remain below one hundred degrees Fahrenheit, the equivalent of about 37.7 degrees Celsius. In Germany, temperatures above 25 degrees are rare, even in the summer.

This brief characterization of Florida is intended to help you decide where you would like to live and select a suitable location for your dream home.

Decide the Right Size for Your Dream Home

This question is relatively easy to answer when you know how big your family is. That should be pretty easy to find out...right? Assume one person per bedroom. The owner couple or parents generally takes the largest bedroom.

In newer construction, normally each bedroom has its private bathroom, or two bedrooms have a shared bathroom that is accessible from both rooms. Such a bathroom is called a Jack and Jill bathroom.

The bedroom of the homeowner or parents, usually called the master bedroom, has its own separate bathroom. This bathroom often has a bathtub and a separate stall shower, as well as two sinks and a separate toilet. Such a bathroom is also known as master bathroom.

The other bathrooms in the house might have only one of the two options—either a shower or a bathtub, as well as a sink and a toilet. Such a bathroom is called a full bathroom.

The half bathrooms, also called guest bathrooms, have only a toilet and a small sink. Such small bathrooms are rarely connected to a bedroom. Instead, they are close to common areas like the kitchen, living room, dining room, and family room.

The common areas of a house are not always explicitly mentioned in the property descriptions on the online portals, but they are regarded as standard components of the building. In the property descriptions, often only the bedrooms and bathrooms are used to categorize the house's size.

Home descriptions on websites are generally similar to the following: "Three bedroom, two bath house…" This tells you that the house has three bedrooms and two bathrooms, which means that the house is sufficient for four people—a couple with two children.

If you only have two children and each has a separate bedroom, that will work out fine for your family. However, if you are on a tight daily schedule, two bathrooms might be tough when you think of the daily morning bathroom activities. If you want to use this house as an investment and rent it out long term (longer than six months), you can only lease it to smaller families.

Know the Specifics About Florida Properties

In American homes, you will rarely find closets that are standing at the wall as it is common in many countries. The cupboards for clothes and linens are built into the interior walls when the house is constructed. These closets are closed with wood or metal folding doors. Mirrored doors are also available, and you can easily change them to whatever you like best. Such a solution is space-saving and comfortable.

If there is enough space in the house, these cabinets are accessible as a separate room and offer plenty of space for individual design ideas on the inside, such as shelving, hanging rails, and drawers.

Furthermore, properties are often sold with functional kitchen and laundry appliances. A basically equipped kitchen has a refrigerator and a stove. An upgraded kitchen includes a dishwasher, microwave, and garbage disposal. If you are lucky, your new dream home will include a washer and dryer too, because drying of laundry outside is not common.

In addition to the above-mentioned appliances, each property in Florida has a hot water heater and an air-conditioning system as a standard feature.

That means for you that you can quickly move into a house equipped with all of the basic amenities. You can cook your meals, wash your clothes, shower, and hang your clothes in the existing closets. Who could expect more?

Well, you will need a mattress for the first night, but you can get this quickly at a local store, and then you will no longer be dependent on a hotel.

As you will see in your house showing tours, most kitchens are equipped with electric stoves. Gas stoves are not so common. If you prefer gas appliances, you should give this information to your sale agent so that he or she can adjust the search criteria accordingly.

Each property has a hot water boiler, but these have varying tank sizes. Tankless water heaters are not yet common in Florida, but when you remodel your house, you can easily replace your water heater with a tankless one.

A functioning air-conditioning system is a standard feature in Florida properties due to the year-round pleasant warm weather. There are two different type of air-conditioning systems available: centralized and wall/window units. When the air-conditioning system is centralized, the air handler is installed inside the home while the cooler or condenser is on the outside in the yard. Such a central air-conditioning system is more energy efficient than the wall/window systems, and it is more comfortable for the occupants too.

Window or wall air conditioners still exist in many older homes. These air conditioners, as the name suggests, are either built into the wall or set into a window. They operate with electricity. These systems are cheaper when purchased than central air conditioning, but they are not energy efficient and they are also expensive in terms of consumption.

A separate laundry room with washer and dryer does not exist in all homes. In some properties, a portion of the garage is used as a laundry area. The washer and dryer are often included in the purchase price, but not always, and you as a buyer have to check it when making an offer. Do not assume that this appliance will stay, because washers and dryers are the personal property of the owner.

The Home for Your Favorite Toy—Your Car

Your car likes to have a roof over the top too. Many properties have at least one garage. This garage not only serves as a "home" for your car but also as storage for lawn equipment, bikes, or hobby materials. Basements are generally not available in Florida, as mentioned earlier.

Depending on the size of the house, there are often two-car garages or even larger. Additionally, there are often one or more parking spaces in front of the house or garage. There is usually no limit to the number of vehicles that can belong to a house, but all vehicles must be parked on paved surfaces and must have tags.

The distances in the United States are much larger than in Europe or other countries; therefore, an American family often has more than one car and therefore needs sufficient parking spaces for the vehicles.

In older homes, you will usually find a carport for one car and additional outdoor parking spaces in front of the house.

…And the Pool in the Backyard

Once you have determined the size of the property you need, the next question is whether you want to have a pool or not.

You can buy a house with a pool in the backyard in Florida at an affordable price. Pools come in different sizes and shapes and various types of equipment included.

The simplest variety of pools are above ground in the backyard. These pools are much cheaper to purchase than in-ground pools, but they are harder to clean and maintain.

The majority of pools in Florida are the in-ground type that is situated in the yard and surrounded by a solid pool deck. This pool deck can be a narrow border or a wider one to allow the placement of sun loungers, table, and chairs by the pool.

The shape of the pool can be rectangular or in free form. If the site has only a smaller yard, you will often find a free-form pool, because this form takes up less space than a rectangular one.

Many pools are not heated, because the sun heats them naturally. Also, you certainly want to use the pool to cool off and not as an oversized bathtub on the outside.

Indispensable for a pool is regular cleaning by hand or by automatic cleaner, as well as the provision of chemicals so that the pool does not get green and become a breeding ground for insects like mosquitoes.

A Private Dock, Please

Do you already have your own yacht or do you intend to buy one? If so, you should consider a private boat dock when you make your property decision.

The private boat dock is the ideal parking spot for your own yacht. These private docks are available in the many canals in South Florida. Such a private dock is an accessory just like your own private pool.

The width and depth of each channel is different as well as the structure of the bridges in the channels determine the possible boat size. The fairways in the channels are often maintained by the respective cities. The cities dredge the canals to a certain water depth when it is necessary. The homeowner is responsible for the maintenance of the dock facility, including seawalls and the bollards docks.

The depth and width of the channels, as well as the length

of your private dock at your dream home, limits the size of your boat, because there must be always sufficient space for all channel residents to maneuver and to turn.

If you cannot find a property with a matching private boat dock, many cities offer the option of parking your boat in your backyard on a trailer or renting a berth in one of the many marinas in Florida.

Where Is the Closest Golf Course?

This question is easy to answer, and it depends on what you mean by the word closest.

If you want to have the golf green just outside your front door, then a house on a golf course will be right for you. You can walk to the tee every day and play your rounds.

But perhaps this is not quite what you want, because the other golfers might eventually begin peeking into your backyard. If so, you have the opportunity to drive to your daily golf round, either to the nearest golf club or to a public golf course. You only have to pick your preference.

In the immediate vicinity of public golf courses, you will also often find many other sports facilities, such as tennis, baseball, basketball, and volleyball courts, as well as public swimming pools.

The Yard Needs Some Attention...

How much work and time do you want to put into your own yard in order to take care of it? Do you want to stay the entire year in your property? Do want to rent your home? Are you in Florida just for a few weeks or months? Do you want to live in a community?

If you live in the property throughout the year, you can take care of the maintenance of your yard yourself. This means you mow your lawn and cut your shrubs and hedges. You also weed and water the plants in the yard and keep everything nice and clean.

If you do not live year-round in your property or do not want to practice body building by way of strenuous yard work, you can use either a yard service at your own expense or the landscaping service of the homeowner's association to maintain your property outside in case your home is located in a homeowner community.

The homeowner's association is often responsible for the maintenance of the exterior facades of a house within a community, because they regulate the overall appearance of the community and want to ensure that every home in the community meets these requirements.

These exterior facades and outdoor facilities include, for example, the roof material, the exterior color of the house, and the landscaping as well.

For temporary absent homeowners, living in such a community is highly recommended, because the entire maintenance efforts are provided by the homeowner's association, and you simply need to pay a monthly fee.

If you are the owner of a condominium, it is much easier for you because in such a complex, the condo owner association provides all services for the entire outdoor and indoor amenities. The membership is mandatory, and the rules and regulations are based on the actual condominium documents.

The payments for these services—in a home or condominium owner's association—are made monthly, and they are charged directly to the bank account of the individual owner. Of course, check payment is possible too, but cash is not accepted.

Preparation for an Emergency

In addition to the already described duties, there are still some tasks left that need to be addressed in case you are absent for a longer period of time.

Let us assume that a hurricane is coming the direction of your property, and you are not there. In such a case, it is necessary to hire someone to mount your hurricane panels or close your accordion shutters. In many condominium complexes, the management company offers this service or hires a service provider for its residents to perform this task.

It is also useful to have a local trusted person who looks after the apartment regularly and, if necessary, empties the mail box and acts as an emergency contact in case something unusual happens. Such a task may be pursued by an individual as long as there is no payment involved for this service. As soon as you rent your property, a private individual is not allowed to do the job.

The rental of a property is a real estate business service, and such a service may only be done by the owner himself or herself, or the owner together with a licensed real estate specialist. Your real estate specialist provides all necessary services, like collecting rent and paying bills, with your permission and approval.

For this task, it is important to select a real estate professional who has a good reputation and the required expertise and skills. A real estate brokerage that offers all these services will be the best service partner in this matter.

House Versus Condominium

You already know a lot about the real estate business and properties in Florida, including the sizes and available features and amenities.

Your next decision is whether you want to buy a detached single-family home, a townhouse or a condominium.

When you own a detached house, you are the most independent. In your home and on your lot, you can do whatever you want, and no one can interfere.

You can live in the house or you can rent it. You can alter, renovate, or expand it. With sufficient resources, you can tear it down and build it new. It all comes down to what you want and what you can pay for and what is approved by the building department of the city.

However, the proper maintenance of your home is one of your duties as a property owner. That means your outdoor areas must be maintained, or else your landscaping—shrubs and trees—will quickly grow out of control in the Florida climate and the grass and weeds will grow half a meter high within a few weeks.

If maintaining a yard is too hard for you, which is understandable, you can hire someone to do it for you, or you may want to choose a condominium or a townhouse in a community and avoid the responsibility of a yard all together.

In a townhouse or condominium, you only have to take care of the interior of your home. Everything else will be kept and maintained by your condominium or homeowner management association. For this service, you pay a monthly maintenance fee that takes away your maintenance headaches.

Other advantages of a condominium or townhouse include the amenities and features of the community complex.

Community owner's associations usually maintain a pool in a tropical landscape. Additionally, you often have an exercise room, with training machines, treadmills, and steppers. In the outside area, tennis courts and basketball facilities are common.

In luxury condominium complexes, you will find so-called cabanas by the pool and sitting areas with sun umbrellas. You might also have outdoor grills for your family barbeque parties. When these condominium complexes are at the beach, a portion of the beach is private property of the community.

The condo or townhouse units include at least one or two parking spaces, either in a garage or outdoors. The parking and the building complexes often have a reception with a security guard who controls access to the community complex and the outside areas.

New Construction Homes or Resale Property? That Is the Question

Several years ago, right after the collapse of the housing market in Florida, it was difficult to find new construction properties. The rate of new construction was greatly reduced during the housing bubble, and the choice of new build homes was limited to a few complexes that were not in distress at that time.

Over the past few years, this trend has reversed, and many new construction complexes that were temporarily frozen in their construction phase are now finished and sold. Many new projects are under construction or about to be.

In a new constructed property, you are the first owner, and you can often select the features and equipment for your new home. However, this option influences the purchase price and, depending on your desires and your taste, will lead to an increasing price.

The benefits of a new construction home is that you get exactly what you want and need in your dream home. The prices for such properties are still at a reasonable level compared to prices before and within the housing bubble.

Already for $300,000, you can get a brand new three bedroom/two bathroom home in a new construction complex.

The decision to buy an existing property may be worthwhile for you too, especially if the owner/seller has already renovated the property and brought it up to the current building code. You will get such a house at a price that is around 27 percent lower than before the housing bubble

(2014). However, real estate prices are rising again, so such bargains are disappearing. You have to hurry to get them.

Existing properties usually have renovated bathrooms and kitchen. The electrical appliances, such as stove, refrigerator, and hot water heater, as well as the air conditioning system, are replaced with new ones. All the interiors and exteriors are well-maintained and functional.

In case the property is not yet remodeled, you have a broader base for negotiation on the purchase price and you have a chance to make a real bargain.

In a current real estate sale market—new or old—everything is possible and one thing is certain: prices will rise steadily over the next few years, and a missed opportunity will be much more expensive.

The geographical location of southern Florida is particularly advantageous because the land resources in this area are limited. The region of the Everglades is a huge nature park and ecosystem, which must and will be preserved for the preservation of the region.

Based on this premise, development in South Florida is strictly limited, meaning that available land is a scarce commodity. The tighter a product is, the more expensive it gets. This applies not only to the land but also to buildings on the land.

Another advantage is the exchange rate between the euro and the US dollar. This conversion rate is currently in your favor, but the US dollar is getting stronger.

On October 15, 2014, the exchange rate was as follows

1 euro = 1.2777 US dollar

Based on these numbers, a property that is listed at $100,000 costs only €78,265.64. In Europe, you will not find a single-family home for such a price in a comparable condition and location. (Compare this with the exchange rate in your homeland.)

These are still favorable conditions for home buyers, and the value increase of your property is almost guaranteed. Properties were and are a safe investment in an uncertain economic future, but the best opportunities are short-lived, and you should take your chances when you can, before it is too late.

Can You Afford Your Dream Home in Paradise?

You have certainly waited for this particular question. You have probably asked yourself whether such an investment is even feasible for you. The answer is often yes. There are many ways to resolve this issue.

With the right real estate professional, you will not only find your dream home, but also the price you pay will be affordable.

With an investment in today's Florida real estate market, you have four huge advantages on your side:

1. Property prices are still moderate, but they are constantly increasing.

2. Today's market value of the properties are still 27 percent below the value of 2005/2006, but they are moving upward.

3. Financing options are back and affordable for foreign nationals.

4. The exchange rate between your own currency and the US dollar maybe favorable too.

Think about these four advantages and adapt them to your home country. Then consider how you can take advantage of these opportunities.

Your next consideration is how you want to pay for your dream property: cash or financing. This question is very important, because both options require different preparations. Without a clear look into your financial power, your dream home project will get off to a bad start.

In real estate transactions in the United States, time is critical, or as they say here "of the essence." If you are not properly prepared and your financial situation is not clearly defined, your real estate dream will unfortunately remain a dream.

With good preparation together with your agent, you can be the proud owner of your dream home within thirty days or less.

By now, you already know so much about your dream home that you have certainly put together your own wishlist and are ready for the next step.

Here we go!

Your Investment into Your Dream Home

To get the best dream home for your money, it is absolutely necessary that you determine how much money you want to invest before you start your project.

The deliberation—let us first find out what is available on the market and then I decide if want to buy—does not work. If you find your dream home and start at that time with evaluation of your financial position, then your dream home will be sold before you are finished with your financial determination.

Interesting properties tend to go under contract within a few days of listing and are sold within thirty days. To keep up in this competitive market, your financial position needs to be clear before you start your real estate hunt. A qualified real estate professional will ask you for such financing information before he or she starts the home search with you.

It is crucial for the success of your real estate transaction that you are well prepared. Part of this preparation is to decide if you want to act as cash buyer or take out a mortgage for your transaction. As a cash buyer, you have a better chance of success in your property hunt, but also a secured funding for the purchase is a good option.

You will need an appropriate proof of funds about your available cash for your real estate transaction. If your cash is still in your home country, this proof of funds can be an official letter from the bank where the funds are held in account. If the cash is already in an account in the United States, a recent bank statement of the account can be used as evidence.

In case you need financing for your project, you will need a loan commitment letter from a credit institution in your home country if your bank does such outer country financing, or you will need a prequalification letter from a financial institution in the United States.

For details in this matter, please feel free to contact us by e-mail. The e-mail address is provided at the end of the book.

As soon as the financial details and requirements are determined and the papers are available, the home hunt can begin.

The Best Possible Dream Home for Your Money

After you have completed your financial considerations, you know how much money you want to invest in your dream home. To get the best possible dream home for this investment, it is now time to decide what part of Florida you would like to live in, because your dream home is waiting for you there.

At the beginning of this book, I gave a brief overview about Florida, the Sunshine State. The information was meant as a little jump start for your location decision. This decision also defines where in Florida your real estate specialist will be found and what kind of knowledge and experience you expect from your real estate agent.

The local real estate specialist has not only the widest base of information for your target market, buy he or she can also provide you with all relevant and interesting data about your dream home. His or her research is not limited to public databases. Realtors have access to a variety of occupation-specific tools for evaluation and market statistics that will ease your financial decisions for the purchase of your dream home.

In the preceding chapters, you have already received some information about the profession of real estate specialists in the United States. Now I will show you how you can use this information to your advantage so that it works best for your project.

As already explained, it is essential to hire a licensed local real estate agent, so that he or she can bring you on the right track to optimal success for your dream home project.

It is important to know that you only need one agent—no more. You may think that two or three agents will find more choices for you. That is a wrong assumption, because each local licensed real estate agent who is a member of the local real estate association can offer and sell you any property that is currently available on the market.

You may ask yourself, "How can that be?" In Europe or elsewhere, you have to search by yourself to find a property or contact many different agents. The answer to this question is very simple. Most property sellers in Florida use the services of a listing agent who has access to the Multiple Listing Service (MLS). Such an agent has an exclusive contract for the sale with the property seller, and this listing agent is the representative and trusted contact to the seller.

Part of the listing agreement is the determination of the commission for the sale of the property and the marketing efforts of the property that are in the best interests of the seller. The commission for such a transaction is currently 6 to 7 percent of the sale price. This percentage is due at closing—that is the final signing of the transaction papers—and has to be shared between the two participating real estate professionals. The listing agent receives 50 percent of the commission, and the buyer's agent—your agent—receives the remaining 50 percent.

The seller's property must be entered into the so-called MLS system within twenty-four hours after the listing contract is signed by the seller and the listing agent.

The MLS contains all relevant and important property details available. The listing is usually enhanced with current pictures and videos of the seller's property. Property details, such as the size of the living spaces or the land that comes with the property, are taken directly from the property tax appraiser's database of the county. This information reflects the latest known information.

Upon the entry of the property into the MLS system, the available home details are electronically distributed and marketed to thousands of local, national, and international websites. With this system, it is possible to update the property information quickly and automatically when there are changes in the listing status, such as "property under contract," etc.

Each licensed Florida real estate specialist can look into this MLS database and may use the information found there for his or her buyers. With this database, a real estate agent can arrange showings for the homes you like best.

Such a showing appointment can be made only with a licensed real estate specialist, because the details for such a showing appointment are included in the MLS system. The listing office is also obliged to check the license of the buyer's agent before granting permission for the showing.

Without an approved viewing appointment, neither you nor your agent are allowed to enter the property; entering under any other circumstance is considered burglary. You as an individual are not eligible to get the access code to enter the property.

With this information, you are now well prepared to find your buyer agent and go with him or her on the treasure hunt for your dream home.

Your Buyer Agent Is Local and Experienced

You already know what knowledge and experience you should look for in your buyer's agent. In order to optimally help you with your project, your real estate professional must be living, licensed, and working in the country in which you want to buy your dream home. Additionally his or her professional expertise should be concentrated in the location where you would like to buy the home.

To play it safe and not get tricked, ask your agent for his or her active real estate license and his or her additional credentials.

The state license for real estate and membership in the national, state, and local Realtor associations should be an additional criteria for your agent. This will ensure that your agent knows the legal and professional rules and regulations and has access to all major and important real estate data.

Start with your evaluation of a competent real estate agent

by asking him or her about his or her tasks in the real estate transaction. Your real estate professional will gladly answer all your questions and explain the details to you.

If your agent does not accomplish his or her tasks and you suffer a financial loss based on his or her failures in the management of your real estate transaction, you can pursue several inexpensive options to receive a settlement for your claim outside the courtroom.

A legitimate complaint can be made either at the local or state level. But if your agent committed a crime like fraud, it will be necessary to take him or her to court in order to resolve the matter.

The penalties for violations of the rules and regulations in the real estate business can range from a warning involving a monetary penalty to the loss of the license (temporary or lifelong). In criminal offenses, imprisonment is possible, but such a penalty will only be decided by a trial in court.

For you as a customer, it is therefore crucial to know what you can expect from a real estate professional in order to protect yourself against unlicensed scammers. This does not mean that each licensee is a cheater, but the risk of meeting such a person is much greater when you are not careful.

In addition to proper licensing, the designation Accredited Buyer Representative is a great criteria for your real estate professional. Such a real estate professional has special training as a buyer representative and represents your interests exclusively.

The abbreviation ABR means Accredited Buyer's Representative and tells you that the agent is a specialist in buyer representation. He or she is your trusted consultant and acts solely on your behalf in the purchase transaction. He or she is your voice toward the seller and the listing agent.

If you are wondering why you need someone like that, think about this: how quickly can you get into a heated and emotional debate? Especially when you want to purchase a large and relatively expensive object—in this case your dream property. There will likely be much discussion or argument about the price and the features of the house, believe me.

To you, a specific feature of the house is worth less than it is to the seller, who has put his or her heart and soul into the creation and maintenance of this feature. A heated debate on these different perspectives can quickly damage the mutual good feelings in the transaction. The whole deal can explode, or at least negotiations can become much harder. To avoid such a situation, the listing agent negotiates on behalf of the seller and your agent on your behalf.

Your agent will of course represent and act in your best interest—buying a home for the least amount of money—while the listing agent will represent the seller's interest—to sell the house at the highest possible price.

Real estate professionals have a detached view toward the product of the transaction, and they have no emotions in the game, unlike the actual parties of the transaction, the buyers and sellers. Therefore, real estate agents are able to reach a consensus easier and faster, and they will resolve emerging problems.

After a successful negotiation, when an agreement is reached on the real estate transaction terms, your buyer's agent will help you take all the necessary steps. He or she will take you through the correct order of the process so that you will meet the specified time frames and deadlines of the transaction.

When the agreements in the real estate purchase contract are made between seller and buyer, you have to follow these terms correctly; otherwise there will be consequences for you and your agent. You will not make it to closing (the end of the real estate transaction). You will not get your dream home, and your agent will not get paid. That is not the result that you and your agent are interested in.

Another good criteria for selecting a qualified agent is the additional training he or she has had, which you can identify by looking for abbreviations after the name of your real estate professional. The most important training for you is the ABR, or Accredited Buyer Representative, and CIPS, Certified International Property Specialist.

Such a specialist is not only familiar with the buying process but also with the various international processes for the transfer of real estate. He or she will give you many useful tips and hints during the process based on his or her experience that will make the process easier and more convenient.

Another useful requirement in the selection of the agent is your language. It is enormously important to have a real estate professional who speaks your language. You will be able to formulate your questions in your own language and get the necessary explanations in your native tongue. This contributes massively to a successful real estate transaction.

If you intend to purchase a property in a resort complex, the additional training designated by RSPS (Resort and Second Home Property Specialist) is very helpful. The focus of this real estate professional combines your desired lifestyle into the search for your dream home. He or she will also explain the existing rules and regulations of the different resort complexes.

If your real estate consultant in your home country made the proposal to purchase a property abroad, then the TRC, or Transnational Referral Certification, is an important additional qualification. It protects all parties—you, your real estate consultant in your home country, and the agent in Florida.

Such certified real estate professionals are trained and willing to work with a foreign real estate professional for your benefit. They are also willing to pay a fee to this foreign real estate professional when the real estate transaction closes successfully. The requirement for the payment of such a fee is that the real estate professional is legally practicing the profession in your home country.

You will not always find all additional training combined in one real estate specialist. In this case, make a priority decision. What is the most important criteria for you when it comes to a real estate professional? And remember, in Florida (as in the entire United States) your agent is paid by the seller. The commission for the agent's services is part of the real estate transaction costs on the seller's side. For you, the service of a local real estate specialist is free of charge.

Many agents and brokers are proud of their training. They have worked very hard for their education and they will be happy to show you their license and additional qualifications.

Think of lawyers in Hollywood movies. When such lawyers meet their customers in their office, you can see all the qualifications hanging on the wall. This is not about self-praise, but business standards. Professionals, and this includes real estate agents, are obliged to place such information visible in their office.

You should definitely not select an unlicensed real estate agent when you are interested in a valid transaction process and you want to be sure that you get what you pay for. An unlicensed person will not be able to present the qualifications described above. The unlicensed practice of real estate is a felony in Florida.

Your First Meeting with Your Real Estate Agent

So you've already thought about your wishes and requirements for your dream home and created a checklist with your most important details?

Congratulations—well done!

You know by now if you want a house or a condo. You know how many bedrooms and bathrooms you will need and in which area your dream home will be located. Likewise, your financial base is evaluated and prepared.

You have also selected, according to your needs, a matching property specialist. Now it is time to meet with him or her in the office in order to specify and coordinate the steps of your real estate transaction.

During this first interview, the agent will ask you for your wishes regarding the property. He or she will also ask how much you would like to pay for the property and how you would like to pay for it—in cash or whether you need financing.

In this conversation, the agent will also ask you for the proof of your financial resources, such as a letter from your bank or a bank statement. In case of a loan, a loan commitment from your bank in your home country or a credit institution in Florida is good evidence of your creditworthiness. This is not different from how things are done in most countries. You will only get a loan when you demonstrate that you will be able to pay it back on time.

Without such evidence, you will not find a professional real estate agent who offers you his or her support. The seriousness of your project is not provable, and it seems likely that the agent is abused as a guide for home showing in the area. He or she has no desire to waste time, which can be spent much better with well-prepared customers.

You might think that this is a bit of an overreaction, but you should put yourself in the position of the agent. He or she is a self-employed businessperson who gets paid only when a real estate transaction closes. All expenses—cars, gasoline, time—come out of his or her pocket. Would you work under such circumstances without the chance to close a deal and get paid? Certainly not.

In addition to proof of funds, your agent will provide you a buyer agreement in which the important facts for your real estate transaction deal will be recorded in writing. This information includes, for example, the names of the parties involved, you as a buyer and your agent, your address, your phone number, your e-mail address, your real estate needs, and your financial base that you want to invest in the real estate transaction. Both parties sign this agreement.

With your signature, you make an agreement about the service between you and your agent. This binding agreement protects both parties—you as the buyer and the agent as your consultant. Payment for this service is paid by the seller at closing of the real estate transaction.

These details are essential for the start of the real estate search, so that both parties have a common understanding of what to expect from each other. Your agent now knows exactly what you are looking for and can filter the whole property pool for your dream home.

The available properties on the market are filed in a database, the Multiple Listing Service (MLS), and all Realtors have full access to this database. It does not matter who the listing agent is, any real estate agent can sell any property that is available on the market.

This approach may seem unusual to you, because you do not have such a system in your country. For example, in Germany there is no centralized property database. But such a database makes the home search for you very comfortable and transparent. You will certainly find what you are looking for.

For example, the MLS database in Broward County (Fort Lauderdale) in October 2014 for the region of southeast Florida listed 11,181 single-family homes and 12,415 condominiums available for purchase.

The price range for the single-family homes was between $14,900 and $139,000,000, and for condominiums the range was $10,000 to $14,500,000.

Not included in this database are the properties offered directly from developers. These deals are only sent to real estate agents who work with the contractors, and these agents bring their interested buyers to the development. In this case, the agents get paid by the development company when the deal closes.

To select your dream home from this property pool, your requirement, your budget, and your financial resources are essential criteria. The new developments have different price ranges and different purchase requirements that you need to meet before you are eligible to buy.

A trusting, open, and intensive cooperation with your real estate agent is absolutely necessary to make "Your Residence in Paradise" a reality. If your agent asks you for certain documents and evidence, that is not because he or she is curious or nosy, but because the information is needed for the transaction process.

Do not forget that when you sign the buyer agreement, your real estate agent commits to confidentiality toward your provided information and agrees that he or she will only pass this information along to a third party when you authorize him or her to do so.

This is the best and safest way that your wish of your dream home will come true. All other ways will disappoint and disillusion you. You will move aimlessly from one For Sale sign to the next. Your dream home will remain a dream and that is certainly not what you want, right?

Your Search for Your Dream Home

According to your wishes, your agent will perform a variety of searches on the MLS database. While researching, your agent takes into account your needs and your financial resources as search criteria. Your real estate agent will show you the matching properties on the computer screen, or he or she can print flyers or send you e-mails with the property flyers attached—whatever you prefer.

Your agent will look together with you at this first selection of homes based on the existing photos and videos on the MLS. Together with your real estate professional, you will make your choice among the potential dream homes based on the available data. After this selection, your real estate agent will arrange showing appointments for the best matching dream homes with the listing office of the seller.

A visual inspection of your dream home is only meaningful when the selected houses or condominiums meet your requirements and your financial situation is sufficient to pay for one of these properties. A little bit further down, you will understand why this approach is critical for a successful purchase transaction in the real estate business.

This action makes sense as the following example shows. We expect the following assumptions:

You are looking for a single-family home with three bedrooms, two bathrooms, and a garage at a cost of $200,000. A search with these criteria on October 14 turns up a result of 127 potential properties.

You certainly will agree it does not make sense to visit 127 properties. Therefore you will together with your agent adjust the search until a reasonable property number for showings is reached. A reasonable number for a showing tour is four or five homes and you can schedule the next showing tour when the first one was not successful.

Once you have visited just three or four of your potential dream homes on the tour, you will be exhausted, and the details of each property will blur together. You will no longer remember the advantages and disadvantages of each property, and it is very hard to make any decision in such a state of mind. On the other hand, I assume that you are not only in Florida to look at properties but also to enjoy some fun and excitement.

Together with your agent, you have agreed on a variety of dream homes, and he or she has made appointments for viewing these selected properties. The agent will also request the access codes for these homes.

To get the access code, a fixed appointment must be made so that each agent who shows the property to his or her customers will be alone in the property during the showing. This protects your interest because you are not disturbed during your own evaluation of the property by any comments of other potential buyers.

If your dream home is vacant, showing appointments may be requested and approved very quickly. Once permission is granted for the showing, the agent receives the information for the showing, such as the access code and where the keys are stored at the property.

If the current owner is still living in the property or the house is rented, a showing can only be arranged with at least twenty-four hours notice prior to the requested showing appointment. The occupant of the property must agree to the showing because he or she is living there. Without such an authorization, entering the property is considered at least trespassing or possibly even burglary.

In Florida, it is common that each house that is offered on the market has a lockbox. In this lockbox, the keys for the house are deposited, and the lockbox is installed at one of the entrance doors. The lockbox has either a combination lock or an electronic opening mechanism in order to get the front-door key.

The combination of such a lockbox may only be given to a licensed real estate professional. When the agent makes the request for a showing appointment, the database or the listing office performs a check with the state database to insure that the professional is licensed.

If an agent does not stick to this rule and enters a property without a showing authorization, the seller of the property and the listing agent can file a complaint with the local real estate association. Based on the severity of the offense, this agent may be reprimanded by the real estate association. I myself have reported such cases, and many of my colleagues do the same thing, because we have to keep the properties safe.

As real estate professionals, we are committed to respecting the property rights of the seller and ensuring that we comply with our current professional standards.

As soon as your agent has requested a showing appointment, the showings are granted, and the access code for the lockbox is provided, the showing tour can start together with you.

Let's Go for a Property Showing

Together with your agent, you have selected a few dream homes on the shortlist, and now you start your tour. Whether you go with one or two cars depends what is more comfortable and how many people are going on this trip. You will arrange that with your real estate specialist.

When you drive with two cars, you should drive behind the agent, because he or she knows the locations better than you do and will guide you from one property to the next.

When you arrive at one of your potential dream homes, you decide what is most important for you: the interior or the exterior with the yard.

If you start with the exterior showing first, you will see very quickly if you like the size of the lot, the view, and the landscaping. If everything is fine, you will go together with the agent into the house.

If you do not like the property from the outside, then it is not very likely that you will be convinced from the interior to change your mind.

In our example, let's assume that you like the home from the outside. Now the agent opens the entrance to the house. The key for the entrance door is deposited in the lockbox at one of the doors. As already mentioned, your agent has requested the access code from the listing agent or the listing office.

Together with your agent, you go through each room in the home, and your agent answers any questions you have to the best of his or her knowledge. If there are any open questions, he or she will make a note and will give you the answer as soon as he or she can get the information.

A preliminary inspection of a property by a real estate professional is not usually done, because your idea of your dream home will be different from your agent's. You know much better what you like and what you dislike, what you are willing to tolerate and what you are not.

If you are visiting a vacant property, the water and electricity are usually shut off. Therefore the lighting and kitchen appliances will not work, so showings should be done during daylight hours only. The functionality of the water and power supply will be tested as part of the home inspection later in the process. In a later chapter The Home Inspection…, you will find details about the topic of home inspections.

On your showing tour, you will realize that most properties have a kitchen with a functional electrical refrigerator and stove. If you prefer gas, you should tell your agent of that preference so that he or she can change the property search. On the other hand, you can usually convert the power source for the stove after closing to your own preferences.

You will see that there is not always a dishwasher and a microwave oven in the kitchen. These appliances are add-ons as property equipment, and you may have to buy them yourself if they are not in the property and you want one.

Further standard appliances in a property are a hot water heater and a functioning air-conditioning system. When the home has a central air-conditioning system, there is a portion of the system installed inside the house, the air handler, and a second portion, the cooler or condenser, is outside in the yard. If a central air-conditioning system is important to you, then you should tell this to your agent so he or she can account for this criteria in the property search.

An alternative air conditioning system in Florida are wall and window units which are are less energy efficient and less desirable. If you do not want a house with such an air condition system, your agent can filter for this critiria too.

Some properties offer a separate laundry room with washer and dryer. These appliances are also add-ons and are not always included in the sale price. However, all the necessary hookups are available in the laundry room, so that you only need to get your own new washer and dryer and connect them to the hookups.

If there is no separate laundry room, the hookups for washer and dryer are often located in the garage, and a portion of the garage is used as a laundry room.

As you will see, the full bathrooms in the house have a toilet, a sink, and either a bathtub or a shower in an average house. In the so-called master bathroom, that is the bathroom that is connected to the owner's bedroom, there is often both shower and bathtub available, and often a double sink as well as a separate toilet.

The bedroom of the property owner is described either as the master bedroom or the master bedroom suite in the property description on the MLS. This bedroom is usually bigger than the other bedrooms and often has additional features like a small seating area for a couch or a chair or a private balcony.

A walk-in closet is standard in the master suite of a home.

The remaining smaller bedrooms usually have built-in wall cabinets for clothing. These wardrobes are usually closed with folding or sliding doors.

In higher-priced homes, you will find further additional features, like a fireplace or a so-called media room. A media room is like a small private cinema room for the entertainment of the family.

Other highlights in luxury houses are an exercise room and an elevator, a bar, and other nice gimmicks like a wine cellar or a bar inside the pool.

The additional features in the outdoor area include a swimming pool with or without a hot tub and a corresponding pool deck for tanning. The pool area is often screened. This means that the pool and the outdoor area are surrounded by an insect mesh constructed to protect this area from the intrusion of insects.

An important feature for boat owners is the private dock. It consists of a wooden structure with bollards to dock your boat and a walking surface for boarding of your boat.

Other interesting exterior highlights in such luxury homes are guest houses, private tennis courts or golf greens, and balconies that are accessible from the individual rooms to ensure the privacy of the residents.

All these properties, with all the lovely accoutrements, are located in tropical Florida lush landscaping, and that gives you the impression of a life in paradise. When the vegetation is densely planted, the tropical plants shelter you from the eyes of your next-door neighbors.

You have now seen your first property. That one may not

have all the features you are looking for, but it has at least those that are most important to you and matches your search criteria. Now let us go on to the next dream home…and the next…until you have completed today's tour.

At the end of the tour a talk with your agent about the just finished showing trip makes sense to determine what property you liked and which one you do not like. With this information it is possible to optimize your wish list and the property search will be better adjusted to your requirements.

You will probably make more than one real estate showing tour until you find your dream home for which you want to make a purchase offer. A little bit patience is necessary to make your dream home project a success and make you happy.

Wow! Here Is Your Dream Home—What Comes Next?

Your showing tour or tours were a great success, and you have just found your dream home. Congratulations! You have reached your first milestone, and now it is on to the next.

Your real estate agent will now prepare the purchase agreement. At this states, the purchase contract is called an offer.

In Florida, real estate purchase contracts are not created and written individually by a lawyer. Instead, standard contracts are used. In many other countries, attorneys with a special expertise draw up separate contracts for each and every sale transaction. This attorney is either paid by the seller or the buyer—this is different in every country. Compare this to your own country's business regulations.

You do not need to be concerned about these standard contracts. They are created and constantly adapted to the current legal base by the Florida Bar Association—that is the lawyer association in Florida—and the Florida Realtors. Therefore, these contracts are perfectly legal and binding in a real estate transaction.

The standard contracts are completely prefabricated and contain only open fields for the individual details of each party of the transaction. These individual fields include, for example, the buyer's name and the seller's name and other personal information like the buyer's and seller's home addresses and the names of both of the real estate professionals—the listing and the sale agent.

Your buyer's agent downloads the most recent standard contract and fills in the blank fields. The blank fields are unique for each individual transaction, and therefore they are filled in separately. The other passages in the purchase contract are the same in every contract and include all the following important details: what transaction steps have to be done and when each step needs to be finished, when the contract is breached and the consequences in case the contract is breached, and much more.

Among the most important information inserted by your agent into the contract form includes the parties—the names of the buyer and seller—the real estate data like the address of the property, the location as well as the control number of the property, the purchase price, method of payment, the closing of the transaction, and the cost-sharing of the transaction costs.

Once the agent has filled in all the necessary blank fields, the purchase offer is ready to sign. The agent will print the contract. After your signature under the contract, your agent submits the offer to the seller.

With your signature as the buyer, the contract draft turns into an official offer to buy a property from the named seller in the contract.

This offer is forwarded to the representative of the seller. The listing agent has the duty to present your offer and all other existing offers from different buyers to the seller.

Due to positive trends in the real estate market for buyers, you are often not the only interested buyer for a property, and you are in direct competition with other buyers. To put yourself in a particularly advantageous position, a fair purchase price for the property of your dreams is recommended. Together with the offer, proof of your financial resources will be presented to the seller. That will show that you will be able to complete the real estate transaction. Without proof of funds, your offer has little to no chance of being recognized by the seller, because the seller is only interested in buyers who can close the deal.

As previously described, the proof of your financial strength can either be a letter from your bank stating that you have a certain amount of money in the account and can use it for your personal projects or a written loan approval from your bank.

In this loan commitment, your bank confirms that it will provide you with a certain amount of money for the purchase of a property. This loan commitment, or preapproval, states at this time only the willingness of your bank to finance your real estate project.

This loan commitment to finance your individual dream property only comes into existence when the real estate purchase contract is signed by the seller. In this case, there is a legally binding contract for both parties in the transaction.

If you start now to gather your financial documents for this transaction, you will lose the game on your dream home. The seller will not wait until you are ready and will accept a different offer that brings the best benefits for the seller.

These benefits may be cash or a quick closing of the real estate deal. Each seller has different personal priorities and objections that he or she wants to be met.

In addition to the proof of your financial resources, you also have to provide the so-called earnest money with the offer. This earnest money will be due when the seller accepts your offer and signs your offer.

The earnest money amount is an initial payment of the purchase price for your dream home. As the buyer, you affirm your offer with this payment, and the higher this down payment or earnest money is, the more weight it carries to help you get a positive response from the seller. I do not know if this business habit is common in your home country and if it is essential in your country, but in Germany it is not common.

As the earnest money amount is 10 percent of the purchase price recommended, with the offer your agent will require the transfer of an amount of $2,000 to $5,000 in the form of a check as a portion of the earnest money. Your agent will copy the check and will enclose this copy into the offer package that is submitted to the seller.

The original of the check remains at this point in the office of your agent. The remaining amount of the earnest money shall be provided upon acceptance of the offer by the seller.

Here is an example:

Your dream home has a listing price (asking price) of $200,000, and as an earnest money amount you offer $20,000. That equates to 10 percent of the purchase price.

With the signature on the offer, you provide a check of $5,000 to the office of your buyer agent. The office keeps this earnest money in trust. Your signed offer and a copy of your earnest money check, as well as the proof of your financial funds, are sent to the seller's agent. The check and the financial statement serve to affirm your intention and your ability to buy the real estate property. If these documents are not submitted to the seller with the offer, the seller will not seriously consider your offer.

The purchase price that you offer to the seller can be a very attractive proposition to select your contract. If the purchase price is high enough, your chances are good that the seller will accept your offer.

Another benefit for the seller will be payment in cash or only a small amount of financing. A quick closing date is another good argument for the seller to accept your offer.

This is only a short list of possible attractive contract terms; your agent can certainly give you a few more ideas. Please consult your buyer agent and make the best offer that you can afford.

Getting back to the transferred offer, which is now evaluated by the seller. As soon as the seller has chosen one of the presented offers, he or she signs that offer. Now there is a legally binding contract for both parties, buyer and seller.

This contract is similar to a notarized agreement in Europe. You will certainly know how real estate contracts are processed in your country. Your agent will get back to you with the seller's signed contract and will provide it to you.

Once the seller has accepted your offer, you can look forward to the closing. You have taken the first hurdle, and you are on the right track to your dream home closing in Florida.

Sometimes the purchase price you have offered is not high enough for the seller. Maybe you tried to save a little bit of your money, and the offered purchase price is below the seller's expectations. This method may be OK from your point of view, but the seller is not obligated to accept your offer.

In such a case, the seller may come back with a counter offer, and now the negotiations start and move on until both parties agree to a specific purchase price.

Here is an example:

Your dream home is listed on the market for $200,000, and you as the buyer want to pay only $180,000. You put that price into the purchase offer.

For the seller, that offered purchase price is too low. The seller counters your offer with $190,000 as the purchase price. You now have three options:

1.   accept the seller's counter offer

2.   terminate the transaction

3.   counter again

If you accept the countered purchase price from the seller, the offer will be adapted and signed by the seller. Now the transaction moves on based on the new, higher purchase price.

Your second option is that you do not accept the new purchase price. In this case, the offer will be canceled and you get your earnest money back from the office of your buyer agent. The seller and you as the buyer have no binding obligations and go different ways. There are no futher activities in this transaction.

In the third option, the negotiations about the purchase price begin. For you, perhaps the purchase price of $190,000 is too high, but you would be agreeable to a price of $187,000. In this case, your agent communicates this new price of $187,000 to the seller's side and hopes that the seller will accept this amount.

The negotiations go on until a consensus is achieved or the transaction is terminated by either of the parties.

In our example, we assume that you accept the counter offer of the seller and the seller signs the offer. Now we have a legally binding contract between the seller and you as the buyer.

With this binding contract for both sides, the countdown to the closing starts and the clock is ticking. In the real estate this is called *time is of the essence*.

The common time frame for a transaction is thirty days. This time frame starts as soon as both contract parties have signed the contract and ends when the closing documents are signed on the closing date, the keys to the property are transferred to the buyer, and the purchase price is paid to the seller.

Thirty days may sound like a long time, but during this time you have to complete several deterministic steps with attached deadlines that will lead to you being a happy dream home owner at the end.

You certainly only want to pay your hard-earned money for a property that has no or only little structural defects and no liens on the title. To ensure these requirements, there are various activities and research to be done.

Let us return to our example. You and the seller have agreed in the contract upon the purchase price of $190,000 for your dream home. The purchase contract was concluded on October 15, and the closing of the real estate transaction is planned for November 15—thirty days after signing the contract.

On Your Mark, Get Set, Go: Your Transaction Clock Is Ticking

Besides the purchase price, you have agreed with the seller in the contract on the title company Title-ABC (this is a fictitious title company for our example). This title company performs the legal review of the real estate documents and acts as trustee for the funds in the transaction.

You are probably wondering what a title company is. Let us make a brief detour here. A title company assumes some functions that are performed by attorneys in other countries, perhaps also in your home country. These attorneys certify the transfer of a real estate property and examine the attached documents to the property at the land registry, the courts, and so on.

The certificate and the documents that represent the ownership of a property and the associated land or grounds is called the title in the United States, which is why such companies are referred to as a title company.

In Florida, title companies don't just take over matters related to the title; they also administer the funds in the real estate transaction.

In other countries, such as Germany, attorneys do all the title work and related matters. They write the contract and read it to the seller and buyer during a meeting. The attorney takes care of the legal transfer of the property, but he or she does not take funds into escrow. The money is paid directly to the seller or the bank when a mortgage needs to be repaid. In some countries, the attorney assists not only with legal matters but also with the money transfer in a trust account.

During the creation of the offer, you as the buyer of the property have provided an earnest money check—in our example, $5,000—to the office of your buyer agent for safekeeping.

After the seller has signed the offer, the contract of purchase is now legally binding. The earnest money, which is still in the office of your sale agent, is passed on to the title company. This earnest money is deposited into the escrow account of the title company, and upon receipt or clearance of the check the title company sends you and the seller a written acknowledgment. This confirmation will be sent by mail or e-mail, whichever was previously agreed to by both parties.

Now it is your job as a buyer to pay the remaining portion of the earnest money, as written in the contract, directly into the trust account of the title company. Payment can be done either by bank transfer or by bank certified check. In our case, the amount of the remaining earnest money is $14,000.00.

To use our example, the purchase price of the real estate property is $190,000, and 10 percent of this sum is $19,000. A check for $5,000 has already been submitted with the offer, so the amount due is $14,000.

In addition to the earnest money, which is a portion of the total down payment in the contract, the title company needs the buyer information, including name and address, the buyer's home country, phone number, e-mail address, and fax number if available, so that the property documents for the transfer will be correctly prepared and created.

The personal information that you provided will be verified at the closing table with your personal ID, your passport.

The seller must provide the same personal information, and the seller's agent takes care of this matter.

The next task of the title company is the review of all of the property belonging documents, such as former owners, property transfers, taxes, violations, and liens on your dream home.

To understand the difference in recording systems in other countries and Florida, let's briefly discuss the rules of German land registry. Afterward, you can compare that with your home country's system.

In Germany, all necessary and important property details are summarized in a registry in the local court. All properties in the municipality are listed in this registry, and for each property the record consists of the inscription and the inventory page as well as the three different descriptive parts.

The inscription of a registry file is the name of the property. This name consists of the name of the municipality and the number of the registry book, including a page number. It reads something like this: "land register of the municipality Somewhere, volume 12, page 3456." Perhaps this works the same way in your home country.

The inventory page describes the exact address, location, and size of the property that is assigned to the above inscription, with book and page number.

Part one of the three descriptive parts contains all former owners of the property and the land. Part two shows all rights and obligations that are connected with the property listed. Such rights and obligations can be the right of way, the right to put water and sewer lines into the ground, and so on. In part three, the liens and mortgages are recorded—for example, a lien for fixed mortgage from a lender for the last purchase of the current owner.

All these details together are the registry for a specific piece of property and the construction on this piece of land. The inspection of such property registry is only allowed with a legitimate interest and is done at the property register in the local court house. A legitimate interest is demonstrated if, for example, you are the buyer of this particular property, or if you have applied for a new mortgage.

In the United States, comparable documents are available, but the names are different and the storage and registry order form is different. In contrast to many other countries, this property information is public and can inspected by anyone at any time.

The title document is called a deed, and it will be issued by the court after a successful closing. One copy of this document is sent to the former owner and one to the new owner by mail. Additionally, the document is archived in public records and can be viewed online by anyone. You can print a copy of this document at any time.

The inscription—that's the name of the property—is a twelve-digit serial number in Florida. This sequence number is used for all of the relevant property documents and papers. Based on this twelve-digit number, all respective documents are always attributed to a particular property. Besides this twelve-digit number, each document has an assigned book and page number, but the book and page numbers are based on the document creation date. Each of these documents is kept in a different physical storage place, archived as the prior documents of the property.

The twelve-digit serial number is unique and does not change. It is also used for the annual calculation of property taxes. Based on this twelve-digit number, it is easy to figure out in which part of the county the property is located.

Now back to the title company. This company is gathering information about the former owners and checking that all previous transfers of the property have been done properly in accordance with the law and that they are correctly archived.

In this context, it is important that, for example, the land transfers were carried out correctly in a probate and in divorce cases. The property rights must be adjusted according to the court orders of any existing divorce papers or the will of the deceased owner, and that the current owner must have all rights for the sale. Documentation errors can lead to delays in the closing date or even kill the deal. In such a case, the title is called "dirty" or "cloudy."

Such titles involve risks to the new owner, and therefore more intensive work and clarification are needed. In such cases, it is recommended that a buyer seek advice from a real estate attorney to evaluate the possible risks for you as the new owner of the property.

During the further investigation of the title, all public records listed in court are searched and evaluated. Then the property is checked for liens, code violations, and open building permits that may still exist and needed to be closed out and paid before the property can be transferred.

An example for rights on a property in Florida is the access to the power poles and water and drainage pipes that are on the property. This part of the land is owned by the seller but the the power company or the water company have the right to pass and work on these portion of the the property ground. These rights must be accepted by the property owners, just like in your home country, otherwise you will not be able to get water and power. Without water and power a property is uninhabitable.

During the title evaluation, the title company also checks that all bills for water, sewer, and power are paid by the current owner. If this is not the case, the open balances must be paid by the seller at the closing. The seller's responsibility for these costs ends at the closing table and yours as the buyer starts at that moment. In our example this moment happens on November 15.

Further charges on a property, for example, are liens from the lender. Such a lien serves as a security for a mortgage and is registered in the public records. Personal loans from a family member can also be registered as a lien. All these liens are part of the closing statements, and they need to be paid off before or at closing from the seller.

If the current owner has not paid his or her property taxes or income tax, these obligations become a lien on the property too and are published in the public records in the courthouse.

A craftsman who performed a job at the seller's house and has not been paid yet can enter a lien on the property. Other liens may arise in the context of a medical treatment of the seller, a penalty imposed by the city because the current owner has not mowed the lawn in violation of city code, a penalty for a homeowner who has altered the property without a proper permit and has violated the building code, and so on.

The title company checks all these charges and makes sure that all known liens will be paid off and permanently deleted from the records prior to the closing of your real estate transaction.

Next, a so-called title abstract is created. This is a document of three to five pages in which the results of the title investigation are described in detail. This document gives a clear picture of the real estate property that you are buying.

Based on the results of the title investigation, the title is either clean, or without any issues that could hurt your owner rights, or dirty (or cloudy), which means there are some issues that might hurt your rights.

The investigation results determine whether a title insurance for your dream home is possible or not. The title insurance covers the real estate buyer against any undocumented or floating and open claims against the current and former owners.

This means for you, if anyone tries to enter a lien on your dream home in the future and the previous owner is the debtor for this lien, then the title insurance company will pay the debt and will demand the deletion of that particular lien. As the current owner, you have no obligation to pay that lien off.

For a clean and clear title, this insurance is quickly and easily obtained. When a title is cloudy, usually only a limited insurance is possible, while a dirty title is usually not insurable. There are so many problems connected to the title that no title insurance company is willing to take the risk of paying off a lien that might arise in the future.

The cost for the title examination and title insurance is paid by the seller in most cases, and these costs are part of the final settlement statement at the closing table when the real estate transaction closes.

As soon as the title document—the title abstract—is created, it is presented to the buyer for approval. This title presentation must be made ahead of the closing to ensure that you as the buyer and future owner are satisfied with the provided title. It also gives you the opportunity to consult a real estate attorney if needed.

If the title is dirty or cloudy, you can decide whether you want to accept such a title at your own risk or not. If you decide that the title is not acceptable to you, you can exercise your right to withdraw from the contract.

If you are unsure about the results of the title review and do not know what the individual items mean, you should consult a real estate attorney, who will explain all important items to you. The cost of this attorney consultation is not part of the acquisition costs in the transaction; you will have to pay these costs out of your own pocket.

If you choose to accept a cloudy or dirty title, you cannot rely on the seller and the title insurance after the closing, because the title insurance—if there is any—will only pay for liens that are covered in their policy and not beyond that scope. The seller will often be out of reach when anything comes up after the closing. You are mostly on your own when it comes to finding a solution.

While the title company is engaged in the above tasks, you should not lie back and wait until they present the results of their title examination. You have to use this time to perform some tasks that are your responsibility in this transaction.

The Home Inspection Is Your Most Important Task

Besides the legal property details, you certainly want to know about the structural condition of your new dream home.

First, your agent will ask the seller agent whether there is a seller's disclosure document or not. This is a document in which the seller provides information regarding the condition of the property. If this document is available, your agent will get a copy for you.

Such a document is not mandatory for sellers, and it is only for informational purposes for you. Your own home inspection by a licensed service provider is strongly encouraged. Do not rely on the self-report just because you want to save a few dollars. That can backfire later.

In a home inspection, the inspector examines the structure of the real estate property and documents all the findings in a written report that includes photos. This report is an opportunity for you as the buyer to cancel the contract of sale due to discovered problems with the building, and you will get your earnest money back.

The main points in this property examination are the roof; the exterior walls, windows, and doors; the electrical equipment; and the household water system.

Based on your purchase contract, your dream home will include kitchen and home appliances, and this equipment will be examined in the home inspection too.

This means in particular that the refrigerator and the stove are tested for functionality—if the stove is properly heating and the refrigerator is cooling correctly.

If your home is being sold with a dishwasher, the home inspector will start this appliance and check if the dishwashing programs are working properly. He or she will do the same with the washing machine if it is part of the purchase contract.

The functionality of the microwave oven, the hood above the stove, and the dryer will be tested as well if they are included in the contract.

The hot water heater and the air-conditioning system will be tested not only to determine if they are functional but also if they have the required performance.

The age of all devices is determined and documented in the inspection report based on the type and serial number on the device. This will give you a hint as to how old these devices are and when you should expect to replace these devices and no longer repair them.

For all household appliances, the rule is that they must be just functional. The seller does not provide any performance assurances and does not replace old devices.

Of course, the inspector will examine all property add-ons, such as swimming pool, pool deck, automatic pool cleaning system, the sprinkler system in the yard, and the private boat dock if there is one.

Another important part of the home inspection is the examination for termites, insects that are common in Florida, and wood damage due to termites. Many parts of houses are made from wood, and termites love wood as their favorite food. This examination is a precautionary measure to determine if there is any termite infestation that needs to be treated to prevent damage.

In Germany, there is a similar investigation performed for wood tick or sponge in the property. Please think about how your home country deals with such problems.

If there is termite damage in the house, you as the buyer can ask for the treatment of the termite infestation or a price reduction—that is your call. The repair of such damages is rarely negotiable.

The home inspector also checks whether all renovations and alterations of the property were properly done, with all the necessary building permits and construction permits obtained. It is also important that all the permits are signed off and closed by a building inspector of the city so that you won't have any issues later on.

If there is an open building permit with the city, this becomes a title problem that the title company has to address and resolve. The correct method of dealing with this particular issue depends on the content of the building project and the status of it.

To obtain homeowner's insurance against storm, fire, and water for your new dream home, there are some additional examinations necessary during the home inspection. These additional checks are based on the requirements of the house insurer. The scope and criteria are subject to changes based on new building codes and insurance policies. You can get the actual requirements directly from the insurer or from their insurance agents. These requirements can vary due to the age, construction and location of your dream home.

As a result of this special examination, you will get a separate insurance report for your future insurer. You have to present this report to the insurance company to get all benefits and discounts that are available for your home and the location.

If this insurance report is done during your home inspection, you will often get a discount from your home inspector on the total amount of your bill.

If you choose not to do an insurance examination during your home inspection, your future insurer will order such an examination at your expense, and these costs will be about 20 to 30 percent more expensive. You can ignore this insurance examination only when you do not want to insure your new dream home and pay cash for the property. To take such a risk is not very wise, because in case of a fire or a storm damage, you will have to pay for all the damages yourself.

The home inspection and insurance inspection are necessary to protect you as the new homeowner from any damages that are not obviously noticeable. The expenses for these inspections are paid by the buyer; that means you. These costs are not part of the closing costs and have to be paid separately.

In the home inspection report, the house inspector describes all the deficiencies of the property and recommends an appropriate solution. The costs for the recommended solution are estimates and serve only as a guide for you. The actual cost will be determined when you hire a craftsman or a licensed contractor to do the recommended work and ask for an estimate for the work and the materials.

The estimates for the deficiency repairs are a good indicator for you to negotiate the purchase price after the inspection is done. Your real estate agent can try to put these estimated expenses or at least part of them on the seller and ask for a price reduction. However, there is no guarantee that you and your agent will be successful.

Let us assume in our example that your dream home has a little roof damage, and this damage results in a moisture stain in one of the bedrooms.

The moisture damage is visible in the bedroom as a stain on the ceiling, but the cause of this stain is not exactly known because the home inspector has no permission to investigate the cause by damaging the ceilings and walls. The home inspector simply reports the facts—moisture—and an approximate cost estimate based on his or her experience.

In our example, the home inspector will only inspect the roof in the appropriate spot on the outside and then document the facts and technical expertise and business knowledge.

This expertise could indicate that the roof covering is damaged. As a result, water has come into the house, damaged the roof insulation, and caused ceiling damage. His or her estimated repair cost for this problem is calculated in our example as $300 to $1,000, depending on the cause, which you will find out when the repair is done.

As the future property owner, you have the opportunity to ask the seller to repair this damage without changing the purchase price, or you can insist on a purchase price reduction in the amount of the estimated damages.

The seller has two options: he or she can fulfill your request or disagree.

If the seller rejects your request, you as a buyer have the option to withdraw from the existing sales contract and get your earnest money back. You do not have to give any reasons to the seller for your withdrawal.

If the seller decides to accept your request for the price reduction, the purchase price in the existing contract will be adjusted and the real estate transaction will move on without any interruption toward the closing.

For such a home inspection, there is a specific timeline in the real estate purchase contract, and this timeline is normally five to ten days. This time period starts to run when the contract is signed and is legally binding for both parties, the seller and the buyer.

In our example, the beginning of the inspection period is October 15, and it ends ten days later.

If you do not perform the home inspections within the permitted time limit or you refrain entirely from the inspection, you accept the property in its actual condition, and you have no right to cancel the purchase contract due to construction defects or building problems.

If you do try to get out of the contract based on home inspection results after the inspection period, you might breach the contract, and you will lose your earnest money when you do not close the real estate transaction. In this specific case it is highly recommended to consult a real estate attorney before you act.

Now Let's Talk About the Money—Cash or Financing

As a buyer, you have already successfully accomplished some very important steps in the real estate transaction. The home inspection is either ordered or finished, and the title examination is in process.

Now it is time to take care of the money matters that you have offered in your purchase contract of your dream home to seller.

With the signature under the purchase agreement, you have determined whether you are a cash payer or you will use financing for the purchase of your dream home.

Let us start with the cash payment option for your dream home. When you began with the dream home search, your real estate agent asked you for your financial funds and the related documents—bank statements or bank letter—as proof.

You've already paid your earnest money—in our example it was $19,000 for a purchase price of $190,000—into the trust account of the title company. This is the down payment of 10 percent and a part of the total purchase price.

Now it is time to get the remaining 90 percent of the purchase price and your part of the necessary closing costs ready—details about these costs are described in the chapter The Closing Settlement Statement. This portion of the money needs to be transferred into the escrow account of the title company before the scheduled closing date.

Your task is to provide the rest of the purchase price money, and this task depends upon where your money is deposited. If the money is still in your home country, it is time to transfer it into your account in the United States or directly into the escrow account of the title company.

If your money is already in your account in the United States, then you have to talk to your bank clerk and arrange the money transfer from your bank account to the escrow account of the title company.

Please keep in mind that trustworthy and competent title companies will not accept any private checks or cash money that is provided in a briefcase. In this case, the title company might get in legal trouble because with such cash sums illegal businesses are suspected, such as money laundering or drug money.

If the title company accepts a bank certified check, this check must be submitted early enough so that the title company gets the check and can cash this guaranteed money from the bank at least two to three days before the scheduled closing date.

In our example, the closing date is November 15, and the money should be in the escrow account of the title company a few days before that date. Be sure to take into your time calculation possible Sundays and holidays.

You may be wondering why this is necessary. In the United States, large cash amounts, as bank notes or checks, are generally suspicious and reported to a government agency due to the Money Laundering Act. This rule is valid for every money transfer from a foreign country.

If you bring cash or financial papers into the United States that exceed the sum of $10,000, you are obligated to declare this money at your point of entry.

The point of entry for you is the desk of the Border Patrol and Homeland Security at the airport. In Florida, this is mainly the Miami airport, which is the first point at which most visitors to the state enter into the United States.

If you do not declare the funds, you are liable to prosecution. The punishment can be very hard and may cost you more than you are willing to pay. Believe me, it is not worth taking such a risk. The declaration of the money is very simple on your Customs Declaration that you get in the aircraft before the plane lands, and it has no consequences for you.

To avoid all these problems, it is worth it to move the money with a wire transfer from your home country to the United States.

You are surely interested to know how you can earn on currency conversion and transfer of your money and how you can take advantage of the currency fluctuations like the big companies do. With a smart and timely preparation, this is easy to achieve. This kind of money transfer is legal and safe and is performed by specilized companies. However, when you have a strict and tight deadline for the money transfer like a closing date this is not an option for you.

Full discussion of this topic is beyond the scope of this book. To get some details on this topic, please contact us by e-mail. The e-mail address is at the end of the book.

Let us come now to the financing option in the real estate contract. This option has some peculiarities that must be addressed and requires more time for the proper and safe execution.

If the purchase of your dream home is dependent on financing, this matter must be your first priority when buying a home. You should already start your first activity before you even start the house search, because this option requires time-consuming documentation for the loan application. You need to get documents from your home bank and your accountant that explain your income situation and your expenses.

You might say it makes no sense for you to provide a credit application if you do not know how much money you will need. Unfortunately, that is not the right approach for this matter. It does make sense to discuss this issue with a finance service provider and find out how much that lender will grant you for a loan. Only with this information will your dream home project be meaningful and successful.

If you select the financing option in the purchase contract with the seller, you have entered into a timed commitment for the mortgage application. That means that in regards to your sales agreement you have only a very narrow time frame for the mortgage application It is also your obligation to inform the seller promptly about your financing approval.

If you cannot keep this time frame, for example because you are unable to collect all the documents for the financing application, this may be a breach of the purchase contract and in the worst case you can lose your earnest money. You certainly do not want to risk that, so you should make sure you are prequalified by a lender before making the purchase offer to the seller.

There are two kinds of loan officers in the business: independent mortgage brokers and mortgage or loan officers.

Independent mortgage brokers are not connected to a specific financial institution or lender. They work with many different banks, lenders, and private money lenders. Mortgage or loan officers are employed by a bank—for example, Bank of America, and their performed function is to generate new loans for their employers and do all the necessary steps for the installment of the loan.

A prequalification means nothing other than that you have talked to a financing professional about your income and financial circumstances. It is important for this officer to know how much you earn and what expenses and obligations you have each month. The remaining free available amount of money can be used for the loan payments in the future in the United States.

At this point, the bank also determines the maximum possible amount of financing for your dream home. For a non-American, the financing ratio for a property is in the best case 70 percent of the purchase price. That means you will be able to finance 70 percent and you have to make a down payment out of your pocket of 30 percent.

This calculation gives you a reliable basis for how much your dream home may cost. All these details are documented in the prequalification letter from your lender, and you will receive a copy of this letter for your records. This letter is also used as proof of your financial ability to purchase a property.

You should already have this letter before you begin your property search. You will already know what you can afford and what kind of real estate properties your agent should present to you.

When you begin these important steps for the financing after you have delivered your offer to the seller, you may find that even though you are already in love with your dream home, you cannot get the necessary financing for that purchase price. So you not only destroy your dreams, but all your efforts have been in vain. This frustration can be avoided with timely and proper preparation.

In our existing example, we have a purchase price of $190,000. With a financing ratio of 70 percent of the purchase price, your maximum loan amount would be $133,000.

Smart as you are, you already know that you can finance this amount based on the prequalification letter from the bank, and you have found your dream home in the meantime.

You have already done your home inspection, and you know what you can expect from the building structure and condition. You also know whether you should put some money aside for renovations.

After you have successfully passed the loan preliminary check and you have found your dream home, your financial professional will discuss the different financing options with you and calculate the monthly loan payments.

The financing options can come with different repayment times. Common are loans with five, ten, or fifteen years. Also available are thirty-year loans, but these may not be attractive or possible for you as a foreign national when you do not intend to become a US citizens and keep the property for such a long time period.

You have different options of interest rates. There are the fixed rates and the floating rates, which are slightly higher for foreign nationals than for US citizens. When a lender finances a foreign national, it accepts a higher credit risk and calculates this risk into the mortgage interest rate.

In the United States, there is also the interest rate reduction available when you feel that your interest rate is too high. In this case, you pay a discount or reduction in loan disbursement. The term for this kind of discount is points in the United States, and the more points, the higher the discount amount. The base for the calculation of the point is the total loan amount and each point represents 1 percent.

My recommendation with all financing options is to ask if repayments or early repayments are allowed without incurring penalty costs. Normally such repayment methods are free, but it's better to examine this when you take the mortgage and document it in your papers accordingly.

An important tip for you: you do not have to stay with the lender from whom you obtain the prequalification letter. You can go "shopping" for a better loan rates with other banks or mortgage brokers and can choose the lender that is best for your needs. However, you cannot waste too much time doing this, and you certainly have to keep an eye on the time frame that is stated in your purchase agreement because time is of the essence as already mentioned.

After your financing options are decided, your financial professional will take the lead for this part of the transaction. He or she will collect and verify the necessary information from you for the lending documents. These necessary documents may differ from one lender to the other, but they always include verifiable proof of income, tax declaration, and letters from your bank and your accountant. Be prepared for this documentation.

All documents must be in English. The translations must have a corresponding certification notice from the translator, otherwise it may cause difficulties with the lenders, because their employees cannot read and understand the documents in your own language and will not trust the content of the documents when they are not in English.

You are smart, of course, and you have all these documents with you. Now the mortgage professional will prepare the necessary mortgage paperwork for your dream home.

Before you get the final mortgage approval and commitment, there will be an appraisal for your dream home ordered by your lender.

Such a property appraisal for a real estate property is different from the home inspection, because the objective is different and not comparable.

The home inspection examines the building structure of the real estate property and notes any deficiencies and repair costs. This serves you and your security, so that you know what you are buying.

The property appraisal is a property evaluation for the lender and protects the lender. The costs for this appraisal are in direct connection with your mortgage, so you pay for it.

In the appraisal report, all physical details of your property are collected. This evaluation takes into consideration the building structure, age of the property, and any completed renovations, additions, and remodeling efforts. Add-ons like a pool increase the market value of the house, and the wear and tear of older homes or older renovations deduct from market value.

Additionally, six equivalent properties that are within a one-mile radius are used as comparable real estate properties to your dream dream home. The purchase price of your dream home should be within the price range of these six comparable homes. This comparison of the homes is an indicator for the actual market situation and should insure that you do not finance higher than your dream home is worth. The comparison result limits the maximal possible loan amount for your dream home.

Three of these comparable properties are acitve listing on the market. That means that these homes are actively offered on the real estate market and are not yet under contract. The other three properties are transactions that have already closed within the last three to six months.

These six real estate properties represent the market prices—or better the market value—of comparable homes in the close neighborhood of your future dream home. The appropriate benchmark for the purchase price of your dream home is in the range of 90 to 110 percent of the comparable properties.

In our example, that means that the average market value of the comparable properties in the direct neighborhood of your dream home should be around $200,000.

All comparable properties in the appraisal should either be slightly above or below the average, should have a similar house and lot size, and should have similar house features. That leads to a price range in the neighborhood of your dream home of $180,000 and $220,000. The purchase price of your dream home should be in between these two price boundaries.

In our example, this works very well. The purchase price you have offered to the seller is $190,000, which equals 95 percent of the market value of the comparable real estate properties. You have made a good deal with the purchase of your dream home.

The property value obtained for financing purposes may even be higher than the price you are paying for the home. This is the case when the condition of your dream home is better than the condition of the selected comparable houses.

In this case, you have not only gotten a bargain but you have also provided a better security for your loan financing. On the other hand, it does not mean that you are entitled to a higher loan amount.

Here are a few tips on how to make timely preparation to become a good and creditworthy borrower before you even apply for a loan.

Especially since the financial crisis after the year 2008, the laws have gotten so strict that it is hard to pass the new existing loan application process. These stricter laws are not only applied to foreign nationals but also to US citizens. They have to meet similar strict requirements to get a loan.

The hardest thing for a foreign borrower is the lack of credit history in the United States. For example, in Germany there is a company called Schufa that monitors credit histories, but only for Germany. In addition to the Schufa, many banks have their own credit scoring system that can determine the creditworthiness of their customers due to the account activity in their own bank. Maybe you have similar credit monitoring in your home country.

All these methods do not exist in the United States in this form. In the United States, the banks work with the credit history that is monitored from three different companies. The current credit history is determined on the basis of your payment habits and the use of your US credit card as well as your account management.

Once you open an account in the United States, it is recommended to begin building your credit history. You never know when and for what purpose you will need your credit history in the future.

A good option to start your credit history is a prepaid and secured credit card.

If you want to know how you can get such a credit card and more details on this topic, you are welcome to contact us by e-mail. Our e-mail address is at the end of this book.

All your account activities and your credit card use are documented by three independently operating credit-monitoring bureaus. Each credit card charge and each credit request is recorded for your safety and is used for your credit history. You have to keep an eye on all three credit reports because every lender, bank or vendor has its favorite credit bureau that they use for the business with you.

As the account owner, you are entitled to obtain a free credit report from these credit-monitoring companies once a year so that you can check if all documented information in these credit reports is correct and valid.

Such a credit report is very important and makes your life in the United States much easier. A high credit score will entitle you to better mortgage interest rates and increase the likelihood for a loan.

You might wonder why we are taking this little excursion into this financial area. That is quite easy. Often the desire to buy a dream home grows slowly in your mind. During this time, you can take many steps to build your credit history, even when you do not live permanently in the United States. In the end, these preparations will pay off in better credit conditions and a faster processing of your mortgage application.

Your credit history is only one piece in the loan process. The presentation of the necessary documents and certificates is the second part of getting loan approval in the United States. Once all documents are complete, the loan documents will be prepared for the payment on the closing date. This document package will be sent to the title company.

The signing of the loan documents is done directly at the closing table, in the location of the title company, and not at the lender location. In fact, you become the borrower with your signature on the closing papers and the loan documents, and not before.

The loan documents consist of the loan contract and the so-called note. The loan agreement contains all important information on conditions and payment arrangements, the security for the loan amount, and the procedure for what happens if you do not pay your monthly mortgage payment. You will know that from your own home country.

The note is a document about three or four pages long in which you, the borrower, take personal liability and promise to repay the loan as agreed. In many countries, such a personal liability clause is directly included in the mortgage agreement and the terms and conditions of the mortgage contract.

Separate fees for registration in the public records are due for both loan documents, mortgage contract and note. The amount of this fee depends on the amount of the loan and they are part of the closing costs that are payable by the buyer at the closing date. All of these contract costs are listed in the settlement document of the transaction at the closing. You can find these costs in the settlement document under your name or in the borrower column.

The lender and the title company make the arrangement for the transfer of the necessary mortgage documents and the money transfer. The title company monitors the timely provision of the money and the necessary papers for the closing date.

Without the full submission of all documents and funds, there will be no closing. Therefore, it is very important that all persons involved are constantly in contact and resolve and eliminate the obstacles that may occur in a timely manner.

Perhaps you may think that this is too complicated and you want to finance your dream home in your home country instead. In that case, you will enter into the real estate transaction as a cash buyer, and you do not have to make a time-consuming loan application in the United States.

Under current conditions, however, it is very unlikely that a lender in your home country will be willing to finance a property in the United States because of the legal differences and complications involved in getting the money back if you default on the loan.

In order to obtain the necessary funds for buying your dream home in Florida, you can borrow against your real estate property in your home country and then use that money to buy your property in Florida. However, you should inform your credit institution accordingly about the use of this mortgage money.

In this case, please keep in mind that all activities must be started early in your home country and must be completed in a timely manner so that the loan amount is credited to the trust account of the title company at closing. Please also take into account the transfer activities and the required time for such transfers.

As already mentioned, you must make sure that the funds that are needed to pay for your dream home are in the escrow account of the title company at least three days before the scheduled closing date, otherwise your real estate transaction cannot close on the scheduled date.

Congratulations!

You have now prepared all necessary activities for the financing or the payment of your dream home and can relax for this part of the real estate transaction. The title company will complete the details and necessary steps together with your buyer agent and the listing agent.

The Survey

Another important activity for you is surveying the land your property is built on. This survey determines where exactly your lot is located and how big it is.

You should have similar administrations in your own home country that make the land registry about the location and the size because otherwise the transfer of a specific property will be very difficult.

It is simple in Germany to pick up a copy of these survey documents at the local administration authority. A survey in Germany usually consists of two or three pages where the exact location of the property and the existing building with the correct length measurements is shown. The description is done on the basis of city names and district names and parcel designation descriptions. To define the boundary of the property accurately, the document also contains the exact location of the boundary marker stones, the size of the piece of land, and the size and location of a building constructed on the land. The property information should be consistent with the information at the registry at the courthouse. Please compare this with your own country.

The corresponding counterparts in Florida for city and districts are township, block, and section. The plot or lot limitations are iron rods that are nailed into the ground at the plot corners.

In Florida, there is no central administration for these documents, and every property owner gets his or her own land surveyed when buying a real estate property. The process is called doing a survey.

To get such a survey document for the physical data of your dream home, you must hire a land surveying company at your own expense.

This company measures the plot in terms of the exact size and the endpoints at the lot corners. When a boundary rod is missing, they can replace it and document any boundary ambiguities, for example when a neighbor has built a fence on your property.

This whole process is called creating a survey, and it is documented with corresponding paperwork. The preparation of this document is the responsibility of the buyer, and you pay for this survey. It is in your own interest as a buyer to order this survey in order to know exactly what you are buying; you must do it before the closing.

The title company will also advise you to do a survey, and you can decide whether you want to order the survey on your own or whether the title company should take care of scheduling it.

A survey is not mandatory for the successful closing of a transaction. However, when you do not order a survey to verify the property data—lot size and location—you as the buyer cannot make any claims regarding these data toward the seller after the closing. You have accepted the property at closing as you have seen it.

Special Circumstances That Might Influence a Real Estate Transaction

The above transaction description is a common real estate purchase without any specialties. However, there are some things you should know because they can cause delays in the transaction proceedings.

Homeowner or Condominium Owner Associations

If your dream home is located in a community—as already described, such communities are administrated by home or condominium owner associations—it is necessary to get approval for the real estate transaction and the new owner.

The reason for this approval is that the homeowners or condominium owners jointly own the grounds and the common areas, and they are committed jointly for the maintenance of these parts of the community.

This maintenance is funded by monthly payments from each owner. To secure this maintenance obligation, each owner must prove their financial standing and commit to the agreed monthly payments for this purpose. Besides this, you as a new owner have to accept the rules and regulations of the community and act based on these rules while you are owning your dream house.

As soon as you have signed the purchase contract, you will get the rules and regulations of the homeowner's association from the seller for review.

This document package of the community includes the community rules and regulations about the administration of the community, the last annual financial statements, the actual budget plan, and a catalog with questions and answers.

All of these documents will be handed over to you, and you have three days to inspect and review these documents. Then you can decide whether you agree with these rules and regulations or not. After the three days, when you have made your positive decision, you have to submit an application for your approval to the homeowner's association.

For this application, you must pay a processing fee, and your personal background check will be ordered. This background check should return a negative result. That means that you have not robbed a bank to pay for your new dream home and that you are in a stable financial situation and can afford your home.

If your name pops up in any database that is searched during the background check, the result of your background check is positive.

This result is not necessarily a bad thing, because the found information will be discussed with you. It could be that you share a name with someone else, or it might simply be an error in the records. It is recommended to correct existing errors to avoid such messages in the future.

With a negative result of the background check—which means positive for your purchase of your dream home—you will be invited as a new homeowner to an interview with the homeowner's board. This interview is an informal meet and greet between the board members and yourself.

At the end of this interview, you will be welcomed in the homeowner community and will receive a certificate. This certificate is the official approval from the homeowner's association and is needed as a part of the closing documents at the closing table. Without this approval certificate, the real estate transaction will not close.

Short Sale Sales

Another special case in the real estate market are properties where the owner has a financial distress situation. This is call a short sale. This kind of real estate transaction was very widespread after the burst of the real estate bubble. For a specific time period, 40 to 50 percent of all properties offered on the market in the Miami and Fort Lauderdale metro areas were such "real estate in distress." That means that they were either short sales or bank-owned properties.

In a short sale, the seller still owns his or her property, but the owner can, for example, no longer pay his or her mortgage payments. The reasons for these financial difficulties are often job loss or illness.

In this case, the bank cancels the loan and calculates the total amount due. At the same time, the bank allows the seller to offer the property on the market for sale with a licensed real estate agent.

When the property is on the market and a buyer is found, buyer and seller enter into a binding sales agreement. This agreement is submitted to the lender for approval.

The approval of the lender is necessary because the sale price in such a transaction is usually less than the total due loan amount. That means that the lender of the seller must accept a loss and write off the deficiency.

No lender likes to lose money, and therefore there are intensive negotiations on the seller's side with the lender necessary to get the transaction closed. These negotiations may lead to a delay in the scheduled closing. Thus in short sales, the buyer might need a little bit more patience than in normal sales.

The specialty of the short sale process is that the bank forgives the remaining open loan debt and the lender no longer collects this debt from borrowers.

In return, you as the buyer will get a well-maintained property free of encumbrances and with a clean title.

The short sales that occurred during the housing bubble and in the years after were a major problem for the real estate market in Florida, but they are not a big issue in today's market.

Bank-Owned Properties, or REO

Another special case includes properties that are owned by a mortgage lender and that are offered on the market for sale. These properties are called Real Estate Owned (REO), or bank-owned properties. As the name indicates, the bank has already completed its foreclosure procedures and has gotten the title of the property in a court act.

Please compare this to your own home country to understand the proceedings.

Such a real estate property is often offered at a price slightly below the actual market value, but the condition of these properties is often not very attractive. The former owner has often abandoned the property, and the house has not been rented out; chances that maintenance has been performed properly during the foreclosure process are very low.

When you place an offer on such a property, you will rarely be able to get a price reduction due to construction defects. There will be no repairs done by the lender, and you will get the title of the property as it is. The bank will not fix title problems, and you may get a cloudy or dirty title. That means that you have to resolve any arising problems after the closing on your own—open building permits or city liens, etc. The lender will not help you with any of these problems.

You should be very careful with such properties and consider whether you want to take such a risk simply because the price of the property is appealing. This can quickly change, and in such a case it is strongly encouraged to seek the advice of a specialized lawyer.

Before the Closing—Activities of the Buyer

In our example, we have thirty days between the signing of the purchase contract and the conclusion of the transaction, and those thirty days are almost over now. Until now, you as buyer were very busy, and you can already see the finish line in front of you.

You have examined your dream home by having a home inspection done from the inside and the outside. The title to your dream home is investigated carefully and the seller has cooperated to clear the title together with the title company. You as the buyer have also verified the title documents either yourself or with your attorney.

Your questions regarding the title are discussed with a specialized attorney and necessary corrections have been addressed at the title company. The title company has accomplished all necessary actions to successfully resolve the title issues.

You had your clarifying discussion with your accountant if it makes more sense for tax purposes to take the title to your dream home as a company or a trust or in your own private name.

Taking the title of your dream home in a trust may have more tax benefits for you than in a company. Only your accountant can explain the benefits to you and how much money you will save. Your attorney cannot help in tax questions, but your attorney can assist you in establishing the trust or the company in the correct legal manner that will protect you and your money.

Taking the title of your dream home in your own name may be the easiest and quickest way to get your dream home. With all other ownership methods, your specialized attorney will need to decide the necessary legal steps and the timely manner to complete this process.

When you make your decision of how you will take the title, you also have to inform your lender if you have a mortgage and get their approval for this decision. If your company is owned by a company or a trust, there may be additional paperwork involved in the loan process because your personal and direct liability as the borrower is not possible.

If you have founded a trust or a company for your dream home, you have to finish all the necessary legal and tax steps including the application for a tax ID number before the closing date.

The tax ID number does not mean that you are taxed and that you have to pay taxes in the United States. This tax number is a necessary business act for you as the trust beneficiary or the CEO of a company.

Your accountant will explain to you in what case you are or become taxable in the United States. In Florida, you do not have to pay a property purchase tax as it is common in some countries, like in Germany. But you may be taxable when you sell your property after several years or when you earn money with it.

There is an annual property tax in Florida. As a rule of thumb, you can calculate your annual taxes as 2 percent of your home's purchase price.

During the real estate transaction process, your buyer agent will tell you what the actual taxes for your dream property are, or you may have to ask your agent about this information.

The fiscal year for property taxes is January to December each year. You will be sent a property appraiser's letter by mail in November of the current year that will give the amount of tax due on your dream home. From that moment, you have time to pay this property tax amount until April 1 of the following year.

Here is a positive point to note: when you pay your property tax quickly, you will receive a discount on the amount due. The sooner you pay, the higher the discount. That means that when you pay the tax immediately after the receipt of the property appraiser's letter, you can get a discount amount that is three digits. When you pay at the end of March, there is no more discount available.

To explain the calculation of property taxes, let's go back to our example that we have already used several times within this book. In the purchase year of your dream home, you will get the tax amount of the former owner—the seller in this transaction. If the seller in our example has to pay a tax amount of $4,000 for the property in the current year, this amount is also binding for you as the buyer.

In the settlement sheet of the real estate transaction, you will see that the tax amount is divided between you as the buyer and the seller according to the portions of ownership of the current year.

You as the buyer will be the owner of your dream home from the closing date of November 15 until the end of the year, December 31, and that makes you responsible for that portion of the property tax.

The bill of the tax amount due will be mailed at the end of October or the beginning of November, and that is the earliest moment this tax amount can be paid.

In our example, this means that you as the new owner will pay the total tax amount as soon as the bill is mailed. However, you are only responsible for a portion of this total amount, and therefore you get the portion that the seller has to pay as a credit in your real estate transaction settlement bill.

Our example calculation looks like this:

Annual total tax amount = $4,000

This tax amount is divided as follows = $4,000 / 365 = $10.96 per day

The seller's portion from January 1 to November 14 = $10.96 * 318 = $3,485.28

As the buyer, you will get a credit from the seller or a reduction—however you look at it—in the amount of $3,485.28, and you pay the total tax amount of $4,000 when it is due to the tax authority of the county.

The following year, the tax calculation base is the purchase price of your dream home. In your case this is $190,000, and based on the above information, you pay less taxes in the following year—only $3,800.

In October/November of each year, you will be notified about the applicable tax amount, and you as a non–US citizen will be treated like a US citizen and will receive the usual discount on your tax bill if you pay before March 31 of the following year. The amount of the tax reduction is listed on your tax assessment bill.

If you do not pay your annual property taxes for several years (your reasons for this are not relevant in this case), your property will be sold in tax auction after three years of nonpayment of taxes. Therefore, it is very important to pay your property taxes every year to protect your investment.

The property taxes mainly go to the municipality in which your dream home is located. The state of Florida only gets a very small portion of the tax. The biggest portions of the tax amount are used to pay for hospitals, fire protection, police, and schools. All these details are clearly listed in the property tax bill, because every resident of a municipality is entitled to know for what and how much of the taxes are spent in the different service fields.

You can discuss all questions related to taxes with your real estate professional, your accountant, and your attorney once you have gotten the transaction document for your review and your remarks and corrections are addressed with the title company.

Now the last countdown to the closing date has started. At least forty-eight hours before the scheduled closing date, you should get the last and final version of the transaction documents as well as the real estate settlement bill.

In this settlement bill, you will find all accrued expenses and costs listed that occurred during your real estate transaction, and it will tell you exactly how much your dream home will cost you. This settlement bill is final, and there will be no further costs after the closing.

In many countries, real estate transactions do not work this way. For example, in Germany the billing starts after the contract is signed and goes on until everybody involved is paid. That means you first pay for the property, get the key, and move in. Then all the costs connected to the purchase need to be paid separately afterward. You do not know how much you have paid for your home until you have paid the last bill. How does this work in your country?

The details for the real estate settlement bill are explained in the following chapter, and the calculation of this bill is based on our example.

Time Has Come—The Closing of the Real Estate Transaction

You have done it! The big day of your dream home transaction closing has come. You have received the invitation with the date, time, and location for the signing of all transaction documents. You are certainly excited, because after the real estate closing, you will be the proud owner of your dream home.

The last open task left to perform just before the closing is the last walk-through of your dream home. You are entitled to this step, which is used to check that all agreed appliances are still in your dream home and that the bathroom and kitchen are not demolished or destroyed. You will confirm that there is no damage caused by the former owner of the property when he or she left and moved out.

Walk-throughs are usually scheduled for immediately before the closing time. Then, after the walk-through, you go together with your agent to the title company, where the closing usually takes place in the conference room. Normally, the seller and buyer will be meeting each other for the last time.

The closing agent of the title company welcomes all parties involved, the seller and the buyer. In many title companies, this closing agent is a real estate attorney or has adequate training in this area to answer any open questions about the closing process. But he or she will not give any legal advice to either of the participating parties.

The closing agent is an employee of the title company. He or she will explain all necessary documents for the closing and answer questions. In addition, the closing agent will check the identification of the seller and the buyer and notarize the signature at the closing documents during the closing process.

Often the real estate agents from both parties are also at the closing, but their attendance is not mandatory. I myself think it is a good thing when the real estate agents are present at the closing. It is the highlighting finish of all the hard work and the payment for this work after the closing is the icing on the cake.

Once all involved parties are present and welcomed, the closing agent starts his or her work in explaining the different documents and asks for a signature and initial under each and every document. Each signature is notarized by the closing agent with his or her personal public notary seal. With this seal, the document is a legal document. This public notary sealing is equivalent to the signature and seal of a real estate attorney in other countries like Germany. How is this handled in your home country?

It is common that several copies of documents must be signed. For example, the settlement statement is there at least six or seven times and must also be signed six or seven times. Copied signatures are often not allowed and accepted in public archives or courts.

Each party, the seller and the buyer, receives an original. One original remains with the title company, one original is sent to the participating agents' offices, one original is filed with the remaining documents in the court, and when a loan is involved in the transaction the lender also gets an original.

The other documents—title, mortgage documents, note etc.—are processed in the same way with the exception that the real estate offices do not get any copie of that paperwork.

When all documents are signed and notarized, the key of the real estate property is turned over from the seller to the buyer, and the purchase money in the escrow account of the title company is disbursed based on the settlement statement that was signed during the closing. Then the closing is over and each party goes his or her own way.

In our example, we assumed that each party of the real estate transaction is present at the title company. However, there is also the option that you as the buyer close the deal without being the United States/Florida.

In this case, the documents will be sent by mail to you. You have to go with the whole paper stack to the nearest US embassy or consulate. There, every document needs to be signed and initialed at the marked spots in front of the US officer, and the officer will notarize each signature.

This process should be the same when you sell one of your properties in your home country and cannot attend the closing there. I sold my own properties in Germany that way and had to go with the sale contract to the general consulate of Germany for notarization.

Before you select this option for your transaction, please check with the real estate transfer requirements in your home country or with a real estate attorney.

The Closing Settlement Statement

Let's come back to the closing settlement statement. This document is regulated and designed by the US Department of Housing and Urban Development (HUD). This settlement statement is called RESPA, which stands for Real Estate Settlement Procedure Act and is used for cash deals. For real estate transaction with a mortgage there are additional requirements to fulfill and to document on such a closing statement.

The purpose of this specific statement is consumer protection, so that each party knows at the closing date how much this real estate transaction will cost them. This settlement protects each party against new charges after the contract signature, as are common in Europe and may be in your home country too.

I myself sold several properties in Germany and did these transactions while I was abroad. Therefore, I know that after the sale contract was signed and the payment of the sale price was done, every few days for three to six months afterward another bill showed up that was connected to the sale and needed to be paid. This procedure prolongs the sale process for quite a while and makes it hard to calculate all costs involved in a transaction.

In the United States/Florida, there is only one settlement statement at the day of closing, and that statement is final. The original of the statement is long and confusing and hard to explain in this book. Therefore, only a simplified version (Broward/Miami Dade) is presented.

If your dream home is not located in the counties of Broward or Miami Dade, then such a transaction settlement statement will be slightly different in a few positions.

As you can see in the following sample statement, all expenses, fees, and costs are listed that are to be paid either by the seller or the buyer in a real estate transaction. After the closing, all legal activities will be completed, and you will be the proud owner of your new dream home in Florida.

Sample Statement
Single-family Home, with three bedrooms, three bathrooms, one garage
Cash Purchase for $190,000
Closing date November 14

Statement	Buyer	Seller
Sale/Purchase Price	-$190,000.00	$190,000.00
Commission to Real Estate Agents (6%)		-$11,400.00
Taxes for current year (Tax = $4,000.00)	$3,485.28[a]	-$3,485.28
Title Search		-$90.00
Lien Search		-$225.00
Title Insurance	-$1,025.00	
Closing Service	-$525.00	-$585.00
Documentary Stamps = 0.60% per $100.00		-$1,140.00
Deed Recording	-$27.00	
Total Amount from Buyer to pay	-$188,091.72	$173,074.72[b]

[a]Credit of the annual property tax portion from the seller to the buyer.

[b]Credit or Payment to the seller.

Now let us look at the individual items on the statement. To explain and to clarify the principle of this statement, we will keep it simple and understandable by using a cash transaction as an example. The payout of a loan for the buyer and the payback of a loan for the seller will complicate this process and does not help in the understanding of the principle.

As already mentioned, you as the buyer do not pay your agent, the seller pays the agent.

In the listing agreement, the seller and the listing office agreed on a commission percentage based on the sale price for the marketing services of the listing office. This commission is due and paid as soon as the real estate transaction closes.

In this agreement is also decided that the commission earned will be shared with the cooperating agent—in this case, your buyer agent. You as the buyer are not entitled to interfere in any way with this commission agreement.

This is just a side note, because over the years I have seen several attempts to do so. The customer seeks to get a portion of the commission that the buyer agent has earned for his or her hard work. Such an attempt is illegal and may result in legal consequences for the agent and for you as the buyer.

With this commission, the services of your agents are paid in connection with your purchase transaction. The commission amounts are found in the corresponding position in the settlement statement.

If your agent performed additional services for you—for example, he or she translated a document for you or made some trips or errands for you, he or she is entitled to a reimbursement for his or her expenses and the costs and fees for these services. You should in this case ask for the receipt that shows the agent's expenses.

In the taxes portion of the statement, you will find the respective shares of the property taxes for the seller and the buyer. The November tax amount is split exactly based on the closing date.

In our example, the usual total tax due is $4,000. ($200,000 * 2% = $4,000), and the closing is scheduled for November 15. Based on this date, the calculation is as follows: the year has 365 days, and from January 1 until November 15 there are 318 days. The calculated tax amount for this period is $3,485.28.

This amount is the tax due from the seller for the current year. When the time for the payment of the tax arrives, the seller and the buyer will no longer have a connection with each other, and the seller will no longer be billed by the tax authorities for this property. Therefore, the seller pays his or her tax portion to you, the buyer, and this amount is listed within the transaction settlement bill as a credit from the seller to you.

The tax billing that is created and mailed in October/November each year to the current property owner who is on the records. This current owner is reliable for the total due tax amount—in our example, $4,000.

The purchase costs include, for example, fees for title and lien searches and title insurance, which is issued based on the results of these searches. Which party is liable for the payment of what costs and what services is a part of the real estate deal negotiations that occur before the purchase contract is signed. The title company will only list these expenses and costs in accordance with the terms of the purchase contract.

The next important position on the real estate settlement statement is the title and lien search. This investigation is necessary to make sure that there are no open mortgages, liens, or unpaid taxes on the property and that all changes of ownership are properly done. There is usually a lump sum or a flat fee for this service, and this expense is usually paid by the seller for his or her own protection.

In the urgent case when buyer and seller want to close the real estate transaction within less than thirty days, it will be necessary to pay an additional fee for express service. The regular time frame for a title and lien search depends on the municipality where it is conducted, but it generally takes at least two to three weeks without the express service.

As already mentioned, the charges for the title search are paid by the seller when the purchase contract does not have other terms. The charges for title insurance for this transaction are paid by the buyer.

With the purchase of title insurance, the buyer insures himself or herself against the risk that there are open and not yet recorded liens of the seller that have not been discovered during the title examination and that may be recorded in the future as a lien on your dream home.

In such a case, you as the new homeowner are not liable for these debts, and the title insurance will pay this claim and take care of the deletion of this new lien when it is not yours.

The transaction charges are the expenses for the work of the title company and the creation of all the necessary real estate transaction transfer documents, copies, mailing costs, delivery to the court, etc. These charges and costs are paid from both parties because each party got specific services in the transaction. The services for the seller side are often more extensive and result in higher costs.

The deed is the property title itself. This document notes the names of the buyer and seller, the price of the property, and the closing date. For this document, the seller has to pay documentary stamps. The charges for this document are calculated on the sale price, and they are $0.70 per $100 of the purchase price. In our example, the purchase/sale price is $190,000 and the documentary stamps cost $1,330 for our sample property.

Survey refers to the surveying of the house and the lot size. These charges will only appear in the closing settlement statement when the title company has ordered the survey for the buyer. In this case, this expense is on the buyer's side of the settlement statement.

Many buyers order such a survey on their own and pay for this service separately out of their own pocket. In that case, of course, such costs do not appear on the settlement statement of the real estate transaction.

Recording deed refers to the costs that are incurred when the transfer of the property to the new owner is recorded in the courthouse. These costs are a fixed expense and are directly paid to the court registry.

If the property is not paid for in cash but you decided to take out a loan from a lender, you as the buyer should expect further recording costs. These costs are dependent on the loan amount and are only mentioned here for explanation purposes. In our sample settlement statement, these costs are not listed and not included because our sample real estate transaction is a cash deal.

The main focus in this book is a real estate transaction from the view of a buyer, and therefore the description of the expenses and costs that might appear on the seller's side, such as the repayment of the seller's mortgage or open debts, are not explained in detail here.

For better understanding, each amount is put into an orderly fashion and structured so that you can clearly follow the calculation. In reality, it is always recommended to address open and arising questions directly to your buyer agent and title company.

Congratulations!

You are now the proud owner of your dream home, and you can celebrate this event in your new house or condominium right away.

You have achieved your goal: Your Residence in Paradise.

What Is Next?

That depends on your dreams and goals. You can reside in your new dream home, you can alter and renovate it, you can build an addition or a pool if you do not have one yet, and so on.

If you decide to use your new dream home as a vacation

residence, then you can remodel it to your own taste and vision.

Make plans for when you want to be in Florida and enjoy every day at the beach and under the clear blue sky in the sunshine. Walk at the beach on the fine-grained white sand or jump into the ocean waves—do whatever you want.

How about a diving course? Experience the colorful marine life along the coasts of Florida. Maybe you will get lucky and will find a sunken wreck from the Spanish time and with it a big treasure.

You may think that is not possible. But as recently as July 2014, a gold treasure was found off the east coast of Florida. As a finder, you will get a considerable share of the treasure.

Perhaps you are really more in the mood for a boat ride. No problem. There are many boats that can be rented with or without a captain. Or if you still have money left over from your property deal, you can buy your own boat!

Anything is possible, and the best part is, you always have your own home, to which you return and pay no hotel costs.

You may want to rent your home while you are away. Especially in the resort areas, this may be a good opportunity to earn some income and pay for incurred costs, such as lawn care, trimming of the bushes, and annual property taxes.

If you rent your home as a vacation home, then all your expenses are included in the monthly lease payment.

These expenses include power, water, sewer, Internet, cable TV, and trash removal. These costs are paid by you as the owner and landlord from your account. You include all these costs in the calculation of the rental price because it is easier that way. Your tenants will pay a fixed lease price for their rental period, and you do not have to break down the various costs for your tenants.

For short-term rentals of six months or less, you must add the so-called sales tax. This tax is paid in many countries for every sale and is paid by the seller of the item to the state. I assume you have something similar in your country. The sales tax rate in Broward County is currently 6 percent on the total sum of the lease.

The tax percentage is determined by the respective county where your dream property is located. The review of the applicable tax rate is absolutely necessary because different counties have different tax rates. You certainly do not want to pay these costs out of your pocket, so make sure to include it in the rental price.

Here is an example: you rent your dream home for $3,000 a month, all-inclusive. The sales tax in Broward County is $180. (The sales tax rate in Miami Dade and Palm Beach are 7 percent. Other counties will have different percentages.)

If you collect sales tax on your rental and the rental payments, you become tax liable in the United States. What tax rate applies for your income can only be determined by your accountant, because he or she knows your personal tax situation.

Based on my experience, the tax rate in the United States is more favorable than in Europe. To make the same comparison, you need to know your tax rate in your home country.

The amount of tax due is influenced by the deductible costs. These are incurred costs by you as the landlord. These expenses include repairs to your rental property, the annual property tax, marketing costs, and so on. This is just a small list of the most common costs, and the list is not complete.

As you certainly know from your home country, tax laws are constantly changing, and therefore it is very important that you contact a local accountant who can evaluate your personal tax situation and advise what is best for you.

The accountants in your home country are likely not familiar with the tax laws of the United States and cannot offer you accurate answers to your questions in this particular area. If you need a competent accountant in Florida, we can certainly assist you in this matter.

Furthermore, you need a local, trusted person who will welcome your vacation guests and who will take care of your dream home while you are not in Florida. This person will check on the condition of your dream home, order repairs if necessary, and collect incoming rental payments.

Based on the current real estate laws in Florida, such services can only be performed by licensed real estate professionals.

If you ask a friend to perform these tasks, he or she may be practicing real estate without a license, and that is illegal. You certainly do not want your friend to break the law, right?

Licensed real estate professionals work based on strict business rules and state regulations. Their work is easy to investigate by the state if they do not follow the rules, and they can be punished in such cases.

In addition to that, the Florida Real Estate Commission

makes irregular inspections of real estate offices to make sure they are complying with the regulations. They also check the escrow accounts and accounting of the brokerage. These audits are designed to protect the consumer against real estate law violations. The tax authorities do their own audits as well.

Maybe you have decided to use your dream home only as a real estate investment and would like to rent it for a longer period of time than six months. That is possible too.

In such a case, there are some special circumstances to consider. You as the landlord do not have to pay sales tax, and you usually do not pay the consumption-related expenses of your real estate property.

Examples of consumption-related expenses are charges for power, water, and sewer. The costs for trash removal are often included in the water bill. In such a case, your tenant will have his or her own account with the water and the power company and will get the bill directly. These charges are then paid by the tenant.

As a precaution for long-term lease agreements, a corresponding credit check and personal check—also known as a background check—is advised for every new potential tenant. With this background check, you will quickly find out whether your potential tenant is known as a person who does not pay rent and destroys the property or if the tenant is a drug addict with a criminal record. Surely you do not want to have such tenants in your property.

For the credit and background check, the potential tenant must provide personal information relating to his or her financial circumstances and last residential addresses. These details are checked with the three credit bureaus that are also used in the mortgage business by the lenders.

In addition to the financial background check, there is the personal background check carried out on different databases to determine whether your tenant has a criminal record or whether there have been any irregularities noticed about your tenant in the past.

This background and criminal check are a right of the landlord, and the tenant must accept if he or she is interested in renting your property.

The expenses for such a background check are negotiable. Please keep in mind that the landlord has a security advantage from performing these background checks, so it might be a good idea to pay the charges for these checks yourself.

If your rental property is located in a community with a homeowner's association, the management company will perform these background checks, but in this case the potential tenant has to pay the fee.

Monthly rent is not regulated by state law, and the landlord has to set the price. Rent restrictions or rent caps are not common in the United States, unlike in other countries like Germany. Compare this to your home country to get a feeling about how to act in this case.

The rent charged per month is freely negotiable. But keep in mind that if your rent amount is too high, then you may have trouble finding tenants who are willing to pay your rent. Therefore, it is wise to use common sense in this matter.

Also, the termination of a lease contract in the United States is much easier than in many other countries. Lease payments are usually due on the first day of each month and must be received by the landlord on the third.

If your tenant is in default of more than one month's rent, you as the landlord have the right to grant a one-time payment period of one week. If the tenant does not pay within this week, you can start eviction proceedings. The court will give you an eviction order in this case, but you will need to show your written lease agreement with the tenant.

To execute the eviction court order, you will need the assistance of the sheriff or the police. They will accompany you to your property to meet with your tenant. The eviction process in the United States is much faster and more relaxing than in other countries.

For any more details about the rental business and rental market, your real estate specialist is the right person to consult. He or she will surely help you and advise you of the best options.

A Last Word at the End

Do you already feel yourself as a proud owner of your dream home—even when this experience was only a dry run?

Trust me: in reality, it will feel much better. You will have something that you can see and touch, and you can generate income and revenue from it in the form of rent or capital appreciation.

Your dream home can be your vacation oasis, your income generator, or a piggy bank that appreciates in value over the long term. We've already discussed the vacation oasis and income generation aspect of your residence in paradise. But you might be asking, how can your dream home be a piggy bank and continue to increase in value?

Quite simply, if you buy your dream home today, you buy it at a market value that is much lower than it was in the years before the housing bubble in the United States/Florida. However, the market value of homes in the area have been recovering recently. The table below shows average home prices in the Fort Lauderdale region over the past ten years.

Single-Family Home in Fort Lauderdale (average price)			
	Basic	With Pool	With Waterfront and Pool
2005	$204,870.00	$322,555.00	$531,808.00
2008	$119,509.00	$133,948.00	$146,761.00
2011	$100,085.00	$214,731.00	$408,226.00
2014	$150,718.00	$245,511.00	$445,146.00

Real estate properties have the advantage that they increase in value slowly but steadily. A minimum rate of appreciation is 3 percent per year in this business, but after a housing bubble like in 2008, the growth rates of appreciation are much higher.

My own market research since the real estate bubble shows that the average loss in the real estate market values of 50 to 60 percent have not yet been recovered. On average, the market values are still around 27 percent below its peak in 2005/2006. There is still enough room to get into the market and get a good deal.

However, market development is in a steady upward trend, and former losses have been recovered more and more in recent years. This general trend varies from region to region. Therefore, there are still very lucrative deals to be found in Florida.

Increases in property values will continue to occur because available land for development, especially in the southeast Florida area, is extremely limited. The local nature reservation areas of the Everglades restrict the expansion and development of the Miami/Fort Lauderdale metro regions, and these natural areas are necessary to keep the environment in balance. These environmental restrictions will lead to further growing market values.

Another benefit is the exchange rate between the US dollar and foreign currencies. For example, the currency exchange rate fluctuated between $1.21 and $1.40 in the last three years (based on October/November 2014). This means that you only have to pay 160,000 euros when buying a property with a market value of $200,000 at an exchange rate of $1.25.

Please do the math with your own currency exchange rate and calculate your advantage.

When you later sell your dream home property, you may be entitled to a tax-free gain amount. If the sale price of your property does not exceed the tax-free limit and you have used the property in a certain way, you may be eligible for tax benefits under the current tax laws of the United States. To get this benefit, you need to work together with your trusted accountant.

However, when you sell your dream home, you cannot avoid the necessary tax filing to the tax authorities. As a seller, you must file and submit the so-called Foreign Investment in Real Property Tax Act, or FIPTA. This document is also prepared by the title company. It is advisable to consult with your tax accountant to make this procedure smoother and easier to handle. Your tax advisor will know how to reduce your tax amount as much as possible, or he or she may help you avoid the tax payment altogether.

Please do not make the mistake of thinking, "I have bought many properties in Germany (or Spain or Austria); that surely qualifies me to buy a property in Florida on my own. I also do not want to spend any money for a real estate agent who will be less competent than me!" To complete a successful sale of your property, you need to consider more than just performing the closing, pocketing the money, and leaving the country. You will certainly want to get as much money as possible from your sale, but you will not achieve that goal on your own, because you lack the right resources.

The goal of this book is to give you a broad overview of a common and easy real estate transaction and help you understand that each and every dream home is special and unique.

Each dream home has unique conditions and circumstances that will influence and complicate your real estate transaction.

This book is therefore under no circumstances a do-it-yourself guide. You will need trustworthy local partners for your real estate transaction who will ensure that you do not get lost in the real estate jungle and spend more money than you should for your dream home.

The most important partner in this process is your real estate specialist, who will be at your side with all of his or her experience and competence. This specialist will find the best matching dream home to the best possible price for you, and his or her services will not cost you a dime.

For all legal questions, you should consult a special real estate attorney, and for tax issues a competent accountant is the correct advisor.

Each of these professionals is a specialist in his or her business field, and neither of them will cross into the other specialist's work field—in other words, an attorney will not answer your tax questions, and a tax advisor will not give you any legal advice.

On the other hand, an attorney will not search for your dream home and will not show it to you, but he or she can certainly act as a title company or title agent.

You will only get comprehensive legal advice from your lawyer in the context of a separately billed service, because that is his or her expertise.

All professionals work independently and are self-employed. They are not allowed to ask or pay any referral fees to other related professionals. A referral fee for these services is illegal, although in some case a "referral fee" might consist of a bottle of champagne or a bouquet of flowers.

So you cannot avoid a team of specialists and experts as you pursue your residence in paradise. However, your real estate professional is the center point of your team. This person will introduce you to several of the best fitting professionals, and you can pick your own preferred specialist.

Are you interested in beginning your own dream home hunt in Florida?

If the answer is yes, we are here to help you! Our websites contain detailed real estate and other information about Florida, along with the e-mail address you can use to contact us:

- Florida Information: www.florida-informations.com; e-mail: info@florida-informations.com

- Florida Dream Homes: www.florida-dream-homes.net; e-mail: andrea@florida-informations.com

- Author website: www.andreahoffdomin.com

If you are not ready to start your search for your dream home, then we thank you very much for your interest and your attention in this book. You are always welcome to contact us with questions and notes.

In case Florida is not your dream location please check out our additional book:

- Secrets of the Caribbean Islands – Cayman Islands

- Secrets of the Caribbean Islands – Jamaica

- Or our picture books about Grand Cayman and Jamaica.

Many good wishes from the Sunshine State of Florida!

www.ingramcontent.com/pod-product-compliance
Lightning Source LLC
Chambersburg PA
CBHW050505210326
41521CB00011B/2332